The Challenge of Peace

KURT WALDHEIM

The Challenge of Peace

RAWSON, WADE PUBLISHERS, INC.
New York

Library of Congress Cataloging in Publication Data

Waldheim, Kurt.
The challenge of peace.

Published in 1977 under title: Un métier unique au monde; and in 1978 under title: Der schwierigste Job der Welt.
Includes index.
1. United Nations. Secretary-General, 1972– (Waldheim) 2. United Nations. I. Title.
JX1977.A362W34 1980 341.23'24 80-15001
ISBN 0-297-77586-3

Manufactured in the United States of America by Halliday Lithograph Corporation, Hanover, Massachusetts.

First Edition

To my wife, Cissy

Contents

Preface

THIS BOOK first appeared in September 1977 in a French edition written in collaboration with the French journalist-Eric Rouleau. In August 1978, it was published in a German edition, which had been extensively revised and updated. This English edition is further revised and updated to take into account major developments on the international scene.

The decision of Secretary-General Kurt Waldheim to write a book about his work at the United Nations while still in office is a bold one. The disadvantages are obvious. The secretary-general maintains close and confidential relationships with the member states of the United Nations and constantly deals with them on the most sensitive and controversial, international issues. Obviously these relationships, which are the foundation of his work, cannot be compromised by indiscretions or dramatic statements of opinion on this or that international dispute. Much of interest, therefore, must for the time being remained unsaid.

On the other hand, the office of the secretary-general of the United Nations has become an important international resource and one which the governments of the world do not hesitate to use in all sorts of situations, especially those which they cannot themselves control. As the secretary-general himself has said, the post is, at the same time, one of the most fascinating and one of the most frustrating in the world. Thus, the demands on the secretary-general as the world's leading international civil servant, as intermediary and as honest broker between nations, are virtually endless and extremely varied.

Kurt Waldheim has now occupied this unique position for nearly eight years. Over that period, the range and scope of the activities of the United Nations have constantly expanded and, with them, the task of the secretary-general. In that time, the secretary-general has been intimately and incessantly involved in many political crises and a wide range of efforts to control them, in peace-keeping operations, good offices missions, quiet diplomacy of all sorts, in economic and social initiatives of an unprecedented range and in emergency humanitarian operations. It is an overwhelming burden, physically, psychologically and politically, but extraordinary physical and mental stamina and total dedication to his work have allowed Secretary-General Waldheim to follow a back-breaking routine of work and travel during the whole period, without losing either his enthusiasm or his health.

Under the incessant pressures of his office, he has steadily developed the relationships, the techniques, and the approaches that are required to carry out the tasks with which he is entrusted. In the nature of things, the secretary-general is often given problems which no one else has been able to solve and must improvise as best he can a means of tackling them. The job requires endless patience and the capacity to remain undiscouraged by successive frustrations and apparently hopeless situations. It demands above all a dedication to peace and to the principles and objectives of the United Nations Charter strong enough to overcome incessant setbacks, difficulties, and physical and mental fatigue. A mixture of realism and idealism is essential.

The office of the secretary-general as a political institution has developed further and more rapidly than other organs of the United Nations. It is an institution to which governments repair when other paths are blocked. It is unique in its range, its moral acceptance, and its almost complete lack of conventional power.

It is about such matters that the secretary-general has written in this short book. He describes the advantages and limitations of his position, his approaches to different problems, and his personal beliefs and hopes. It is a first-hand and heartfelt account of the role of the secretary-general in the constantly changing and often ominous pattern of international affairs.

BRIAN URQUHART

New York
1 September 1979

The Challenge of Peace

CHAPTER ONE

The Challenge

One of my predecessors in this post, Trygve Lie, once called the office of secretary-general of the United Nations 'the most impossible job in the world'. Trygve Lie knew what he was talking about. But his remark does call for explanation.

To be sure, the secretary-general of the United Nations is charged with some tasks of extraordinary difficulty. In performing them, he obviously cannot make everybody happy. Each government expects support for its own position and is disappointed when it fails to get it. Where states are in conflict, the secretary-general must remain scrupulously neutral and avoid any word or action that might jeopardize his credibility as an impartial mediator. The job seems so impossible because it swings inexorably between frustration and satisfaction: frustration when the incumbent would like to do much more than the obtaining rules permit; satisfaction when time and again his office enables him to intervene to good effect and contribute to the solution of international problems.

The satisfaction is especially poignant in matters involving human rights. Many times, through personal intervention, I was able to save a human life, even free whole groups of people from persecution. Often it is best to keep silent when these efforts succeed, for the states concerned are rarely anxious to publicize their concessions. But on rare occasions the human impact of the event is too large to allow discretion to prevail once the world's attention is focused on it. I shall never forget Christmas Eve of

1977, when I personally brought some French hostages from Africa to Paris. As I said at the airport that night, the overwhelming joy of the reunited families was the best Christmas present I could have received that year.

There have been other occasions when discreet personal intervention helped ease the tensions between states and checked the outbreak of hostilities. Whether by open appeal or quiet diplomacy – or whatever other procedure I judge will best achieve practical results – these opportunities to intercede in the cause of peace and justice entail a challenge that I perceive as both duty and reward.

Such challenges make great psychological and physical demands on the secretary-general: the loneliness of command, the pressures of criticism, the usurpation of privacy and subordination of family life, and, always, the ceaseless exercise of objectivity and diplomatic persuasion.

In that Tower of Babel which is the United Nations Headquarters in New York, where 152 member states communicate their concerns and aspirations in a wide variety of languages and the big and little crises of the world converge, the secretary-general is basically a lonely man. He has a large number of advisers from many nations at his service, but it is he alone who must make the essential decisions. The Charter provides no deputy. He must be at the ready day or night to take control, assess the problems, determine the priorities, issue instructions, and hold himself accessible to delegates and staff alike. His time, his energies, his personal affairs and pleasures must yield to the exigencies of office. His rank may equal that of a head of government, but the corresponding executive powers are lacking. To vouchsafe observance of the provisions of the Charter and resolutions of the United Nations is his responsibility; yet the only pressure he can exert on member states is moral. His strength lies in his powers of persuasion. Even in the case of unanimous resolutions – whether of the General Assembly, which might be called the world's parliament, or the Security Council, which has primary responsibility for the maintenance of peace and international security – the secretary-general cannot compel their execution. The Charter may provide for measures against a state that disturbs the peace; but the composition of the Security Council rarely permits those measures to take effect. And, even then, the secretary-general is not empowered to enforce them.

As its principal official, the secretary-general must also be chief administrator, diplomat, and representative of the United Nations. He is generally held responsible for all that occurs in the Organization, even for resolutions of the General Assembly or other autonomous UN bodies that he has no authority to instruct. No one would expect a prime minister to issue instructions to his country's parliament; nevertheless, the secretary-general is blamed time and again by one group of nations or another when the decision of a UN body is not to its liking. The public, too, is critical. By and large, people are not familiar with the complicated mechanisms of the United Nations and tend to regard the secretary-general as the man answerable for all its actions. He is expected to embody the conscience of mankind and be all things to all men.

No doubt the most important tasks of the United Nations are to prevent military conflict between its members and to settle international disputes. Despite the doctrine of peace fundamental to every abiding religion of the world, it has taken humanity a few thousand years to resolve to work collectively to end all-out war and to establish conditions whereby settlements of disputes over ideology or power or territory might be attained, not by bloodshed, but by discussion and consensus. The League of Nations, created after the end of World War I, was only partially successful in this respect. That institution had a secretary-general also, but his duties were predominantly administrative.

When, towards the close of World War II, a second attempt was made to create a world organization, the founders of the United Nations drew several lessons from the failure of the League, one of these being that the secretary-general must be given more scope to intervene in political events. Article 99 of the United Nations

Charter authorizes the secretary-general to 'bring to the attention of the Security Council any matter which in his opinion may threaten the maintenance of international peace and security'. He is also authorized to request the General Assembly to include in its agenda any item he considers important. I have exercised these rights repeatedly. In 1972, for example, I proposed to the General Assembly that it look into the problem of international terrorism, and, in 1976, I drew the attention of the Security Council to the seriousness of the situation in Lebanon. For reasons beyond my control those initiatives brought no immediate results, but they did alert governments and people to the need for international solidarity. Ultimately they led to some progress in combatting terrorism and to a temporary cessation of hostilities in Lebanon.

These and other initiatives seem to me of interest because they illustrate the concrete possibilities open to the secretary-general. During the 1973 October war, the Security Council decided to send a peace-keeping force immediately to the Middle East to bring about a cease-fire and pave the way for negotiations. In less than forty-eight hours I was able to order sections of our Cyprus contingent to the area and so prevent an extension of the conflict. The situation at that time was critical. Fear of Soviet-American confrontation in the Middle East was strong. The prompt action of the United Nations and subsequent negotiations at kilometre 101 under the UN aegis remain a satisfying memory for many.

Another rapid UN intervention was the dispatch in early 1978 of a strong peace-keeping force (UNIFIL) to southern Lebanon. This was accomplished within a few days of the occupation of the region by Israeli troops and the adoption of an enabling resolution by the Security Council. As they had during other times of crisis, member states responded promptly by sending men and material. Despite several regrettable incidents, a separation of forces and withdrawal of the Israelis was achieved, the first step in the restoration of Lebanese sovereignty.

I mention these examples because one hears so much about the long palavers in the United Nations but little about the prompt, and often very effective, ways it has acted to restore peace. Who else could have intervened in those situations? Certainly not the forces of the superpowers without precipitating even greater conflict! The public should not be so hasty in judging but reflect a little longer on the contributions of this international 'fire brigade' in alleviating international tensions.

The scope open to the secretary-general in the fulfillment of his tasks is both broad and narrow. It is broad in that his functions are defined so vaguely that he can act whenever he considers it in the interests of peace and co-operation to do so. It is narrow, because the secretary-general must be ever mindful of the interplay of forces among governments and of his role as honest broker. If he should seem to sway in any one direction, he impairs his credibility and usefulness as a manager of crises.

I myself advocate what some call 'preventive diplomacy', which has to be conducted calmly, without fanfare. One runs the risk, of course, of acquiring a reputation for passivity, since the substance of direct, intensive talks with heads of state and foreign ministers can never be heedlessly disclosed – but the strength of such diplomacy lies in that very feature. If it goes well, the crisis is averted, and no one is the wiser. If it goes badly, it is merely dubbed another UN failure.

The ground rule here is: the secretary-general should negotiate only at the request of the parties to the dispute. Nothing is worse, and nothing would be less wise, than for him to force himself upon a situation. Successful mediation stands a chance only if it is wanted and worked for by all involved. During such negotiations, I always find it wise to refrain from making too many public statements. These can be easily distorted, sometimes intentionally, and only complicate matters. On the other hand, reticence poses another kind of dilemma, since a sensible public reaction to the initiatives of the United Nations can be elicited only if all aspects of a problem are openly and objectively presented. As you can see, it is a path strewn with booby-traps. If too much is said, the negotiations are in danger of being scuttled; silence, on the other hand, gives rise to all sorts of speculation in the mass media, which can lead to a hardening of the negotiating process. Diplomatic skill consists in steering precisely the right middle course.

Another contradiction in the secretary-general's role is that he is both dependent and autonomous. His success depends mainly on the degree to which he can retain the support and confidence of the member states who have elected him. Yet, at the same time, he must retain his right to move freely among all powers or rival blocs and stand fast against any external or internal pressure that might subvert his neutrality or his allegiance to United Nations principles. An incident that occurred in July 1972 will illustrate my point.

Unconfirmed reports were being widely circulated by the press in many countries that US forces – deliberately or otherwise – were bombing the dikes around Hanoi, endangering not only hundreds of thousands of Vietnamese but much of the country's economic infrastructure as well. Replying to questions put to me by a journalist, I appealed to the American government to stop the bombings on humanitarian grounds, if the accusation were true. Despite my careful choice of words, my appeal provoked a sharp reaction.

President Nixon publicly denounced my statement, accusing me of partiality and naïveté. Yet reason dictated that, as secretary-general, I had a duty to speak out. Subsequent confirmation of the rumours merely reinforced that view. That my appeal helped convince the Democratic Republic of Vietnam of the integrity of the United Nations was an unanticipated beneficial consequence.

Political differences do not as a rule feature such spectacular confrontations. They sometimes manifest themselves in ways that would be laughable if they were not so potentially devastating. Who would imagine, for example, that seating arrangements nearly scotched the Geneva Conference of December 1973 at which the Arabs and Israelis were to negotiate a peace settlement?

It had been arranged for the delegations to sit in alphabetical order around me and the two co-chairmen of the conference, US Secretary of State Henry Kissinger and Soviet Minister for Foreign Affairs Andrei Gromyko. Upon arriving in Geneva the day before the conference was to begin, I was told that some delegations would not agree to the alphabetical arrangement. The Egyptian delegation, for one, refused to sit next to the Israelis. An extraordinary to-ing and fro-ing went on all night. Right up to the scheduled opening hour no solution had been found. Journalists and radio and television teams from all four corners of the earth crowded the closed doors of the conference hall. The first Arab-Israeli peace talks in a quarter of a century . . . and they were about to collapse before they'd even started!

I made one final effort to break the impasse. To my great relief my proposal was accepted. But it hinged on Gromyko's willingness to sit next to Abba Eban, leader of the Israeli delegation.

When approached, Gromyko indicated that he would prefer the question be put to him by Kissinger himself. Kissinger complied, and after a brief discussion, Gromyko, smiling, announced that 'in the interests of world peace' he would accept the new arrangements. The conference could begin.

Scarcely a year later, on 13 November 1974, a similar incident occurred. This time only one chair was involved. Yasser Arafat, chairman of the Palestine Liberation Organization, was to speak before the General Assembly. This marked the first time in UN history that the leader of a liberation movement had been invited to address the Assembly. The atmosphere in the Assembly Hall was tense. Opinions were divided concerning the propriety of the invitation. Fifteen minutes before the meeting was to open, I got a call from the aide in charge. The president of the Assembly, Abdelaziz Bouteflika of Algeria, had instructed him that the chair usually reserved for heads of state be placed on the rostrum for

Arafat's use. The delegates filing in could not fail to notice it. Some protested; others were openly delighted.

Bouteflika and I consulted. I hit upon a compromise that both he and Arafat accepted: the controversial chair, already entangled in microphone wires, was not to be removed; but neither was it to be occupied. Arafat refrained from sitting down and restricted himself to resting his hands on the back of the chair.

That same occasion sparked another controversy, one which occupied the press for days. Arafat, it was charged, had addressed the Assembly with a gun in his belt, although it is forbidden to carry arms on UN premises. Arafat categorically denied it. A later, careful study of photographs taken when he raised his arms to acknowledge the applause showed clearly that although he wore a holster, it was empty.

Long experience has taught me that an abrupt gesture, an ill-chosen word, or an unthinking remark can prove disastrous. As the leader of the international community, the secretary-general must never forget his every word is scrutinized by every member state and heard by every people. During the summer of 1973, I made a trip to the Middle East specifically to establish personal contact with the various governments. The situation appeared calm but was, in fact, more explosive than ever. Once again, negotiations were deadlocked. The impatience of the Arabs had peaked – a fact confirmed by the resumption of hostilities only a few weeks later.

I arrived in Jerusalem exhausted, having slept little during the previous three nights. At a dinner in my honour, Israeli Foreign Minister Abba Eban welcomed me with a toast. I raised my glass in acknowledgement as is customary on such occasions and declared how pleased I was to be in their capital city. Immediately, I realized my mistake: the United Nations has never recognized Jerusalem as the capital of Israel. My hosts, sensitive to the situation, assured me before I left that, as the reception had been a private one, nothing said on either side would be made public.

Next morning, however, the BBC announced that Secretary-General Waldheim had implicitly recognized Jerusalem as the capital of Israel. My mistake had been leaked.

Before continuing to Egypt, where I would shortly be able to deal with the situation personally, I immediately sent word to King Hussein of Jordan, explaining the incident. I also made a public statement reaffirming the well-known official position of the United Nations regarding Jerusalem. But the Israeli media thrashed the issue energetically for days. The Arab representatives with whom I met during the balance of the trip discreetly chose to overlook it.

People often ask me whether the secretary-general's role has changed since the United Nations was founded. This is not so easy to answer. On paper, nothing is altered. In practice, however, two factors have significantly affected the secretary-general's methods, style, and basis for action. The first is the composition of the United Nations itself. Since 1945 the membership has tripled. The original members numbered 51; now we are 152. For most of the new members independence is something recently acquired. Most of these also constitute part of the so-called Third World. Since the secretary-general is elected by the votes of all the member states, he must therefore interpret the will of the whole. No longer is he the spokesman for a limited group of nations that are economically and technologically advanced. Today he must also speak for a majority which, though not homogeneous, shares common concerns that do not always coincide with those of the developed countries. This has contributed substantially to redefining the secretary-general's role.

A second factor is the personality of the incumbent. My predecessors all respected the United Nations Charter faithfully, but each stamped it with his own interpretation. Trygve Lie was an activist and a committed politician – indeed, to the point of finally having to resign. His successor, Dag Hammarskjöld, was a man of remarkable intellect and vision as well as an eminent political economist. Courageous and anxious to serve the ideals of the Organization, he took the United Nations in a new direction to make it a more effective instrument of peace. Yet his efforts, cut short by his tragic death, drew blame as well as praise. My immediate predecessor, U Thant, was thought by some to lack staying power. Nothing could have been less true. This former Burmese teacher was a gentle, meditative man. His Buddhist commitment reinforced an inherent inclination to ponder issues that belied his courage. He never hesitated to speak out in defence of principle – as he did, for example, on Vietnam. I knew him well, since during his tenure I was an Austrian ambassador to the United Nations and in a position to witness the depth of his concern. Once, when we met privately, I remarked on his sad expression. 'I suffer from the injustice of people,' he confessed. He had just read an article brutally critical of his 'non-intervention' in the civil war in Biafra. I could appreciate his pain because I knew how exhaustively he had been using his good offices to end the conflict, but in utmost secrecy so as not to further exacerbate the suffering. Since assuming office, I have remembered U Thant with increasing fellow feeling.

Criticism is the inescapable *bête noire* of the executive position. Criticism that is soundly reasoned or justified can be useful, for it indicates avenues one may not have thought to explore or directions to shun in future. On the other hand, unwarranted or reckless criticism is not only vexing but can also undermine an entire endeavour. The conscientious man of office must nevertheless take note of both: to profit from the one and to defend his undertaking from the other if and how he can. These conditions, 'if and how', spell out the key differences between national leaders and the secretary-general and point out his greater vulnerability with respect to ill-considered criticism. Where they act for one nation, he must act for all. Where they view issues from a single perspective, he must examine each from many angles. Where their policies are generally backed by the people and power of their respective states in the face of external pressure, his must be governed by the inclinations and interests of the whole community of nations. Where they can publicly repudiate a charge, he often must remain silent.

Given the diversity of international issues, and the even greater diversity of sentiment concerning them, the secretary-general and, indeed, the Organization come in for an enormous amount of gratuitous rebuke. The woes and indignations of the world are laid at our doorstep. The troubled peoples of the world solicit our assistance daily, and all too often the press assails our ineptitude. Neither seems to understand that our actions and our utterances are restricted both by mandate and by member states, that our diplomacy must, of necessity, be subtle.

Unfortunately, the misconception that the United Nations is omnipotent and that the secretary-general is therefore in a position to override the rights of sovereign states persists. The disinclination to view it otherwise, despite our own sustained output of information to the contrary and despite the commendable co-operation of some segments of the media, stems from most people's desire to somehow painlessly attain those universal aims of peace, justice and progress that are set forth in the Charter. Some of the less responsible critics who follow international developments manipulate this popular delusion by playing down the fact that UN action depends largely on the political will of the collective membership and on the good will of individual states. That is why the public reacts so angrily when the secretary-general is at times obliged to disregard initiatives that the public had hoped would somehow solve its problems.

Consider events in the Horn of Africa. During the period of open conflict, I was repeatedly asked: Why doesn't the UN *act*? Why don't you *intervene*? The answer was simply that, for various reasons, none of the parties involved wanted the Security Council to deal with the situation or engage in negotiation. As long as the Somali forces were advancing, they had no wish to be hindered by a cease-fire order from the Council. When the military actions swung in Ethiopia's favour, its government was equally uninterested in any international decision that might prevent it from regaining lost territory and advancing to the Somali border. For different reasons and at different times, then, neither side wanted UN intervention. More important, the problem was seen as being internal to Africa and, thus, a matter more properly falling within the purview of the Organization for African Unity, the regional body responsible for settling issues arising among countries in that continent. I contacted its chairman who made it clear to me that the OAU preferred to resolve the problem within its own framework. In those circumstances, although I followed developments closely and remained in constant touch with representatives of both Somalia and Ethiopia at UN Headquarters, I did not consider it appropriate to exercise my Charter prerogative of calling upon the Security Council to concern itself with the question.

It seems unfortunate that complexities like these, which have such bearing on how I may or may not act on an issue, are given so little attention by the media and are therefore seldom understood by the general public.

As much as I admire and vigorously support a free press as one of the most precious attainments of civilization, I rue the irresponsible reporting it sometimes engenders. The captious members of the fourth estate are trial enough. But in sticky diplomatic situations, the journalist who, for whatever reason, juggles facts, misconstrues a statement or distorts events does a disservice not only to the cause of peace but also to society, because his coverage confounds the public's understanding of the issues, undermines its confidence, and hardens its reactions. The hijacking of an Air France plane to Entebbe early in July 1976 offers a case in point.

I had been attending a conference in Mauritius when I learned that an Israeli commando unit had successfully freed the hostages being held by the terrorist hijackers at the Ugandan airport. I made no secret of my satisfaction at the news, for my position concerning international terrorism is well known. During a stopover in Cairo on my homeward journey shortly after the event, however, in answering a question put to me by an Egyptian journalist, I acknowledged that the Israeli action also constituted 'a serious violation of the national sovereignty of a United Nations member state'.

On landing in Europe, I was shocked to find the newspapers having a field day. They quoted me as siding with the terrorists – worse yet, regretting the rescue! My statement had been picked up from a Cairo newspaper by Reuters news agency and distributed world-wide. That version quoted me as saying that the Israeli operation constituted a 'flagrant aggression', a statement I had never made. The distortion led inevitably to violent reactions throughout the West.

I had the text of my Cairo statement, which had been taped, distributed at once and used the opportunity to emphasize – as I did later in the Security Council – the dual nature of the action: that strictly from the viewpoint of international law, the method the Israeli government had chosen to conduct the rescue was a violation of Uganda's sovereignty, but that the humanitarian and moral considerations had also to be taken into account.

The managing director of Reuters shortly sent me a letter of apology for having transmitted the Cairo account without checking its veracity. Reuters also, quite correctly, issued a retraction. And, in the circumstances, it was some small comfort to receive a message from the Israeli foreign minister thanking me for the efforts I had undertaken personally with the former president of Uganda – even before the Israeli action – to secure the release of the hostages. But the press attacks continued, some even going so far as to say that my 'compliance' with regard to Uganda had been dictated by a wish to curry favour with the Third World. The media, especially certain European newspapers, were slow to pick up the correction; some never did. The sorry truth is that once a story is flashed around the world as a major news item, it is impressed upon the public mind – whether it corresponds to facts or not. Subsequent attempts at vindication almost always fail.

The Middle East conflict, of course, offers countless opportunities for taking pot shots at the secretary-general. But it is a situation of such importance and its issues are of such a magnitude as to command only the utmost sobriety. Still, it provides a clear example of the difficulties that await the secretary-general in trying to carry out his role in international matters.

First of all, there are the pressures put upon him by the parties directly concerned. Each, steadfast in its own convictions, hopes to persuade the moral authority of his office over to its side. While he must remain receptive to each party's reasoning, he must also exercise consistent objectivity. This inevitably leads to disagreement and reproach, first from one side and then another, whereupon the secretary-general must patiently begin all over again to reassure them of his good faith. Since he is governed solely by the Charter and UN resolutions, particularly those of the Security Council, he has a duty to implement the mandates they contain. Any side that finds them unacceptable, disenchanted with the whole institution of the United Nations, tends to hold him responsible for the very existence of those mandates.

And that's not all. There are the parties peripheral to the conflict whose interests are also involved and whose views must therefore be considered. There is also the co-operation of all the member states to be solicited, plus arrangements to be entered into with governments contributing men and supplies and transportation to the peace-keeping operations; not to mention the fears and irritations to be assuaged among those who feel their own problems are being given less priority. Additionally, there are times when the negotiations are so delicate and so complex that it is impossible to release any information. This gives rise to querulous reactions, speculation, and fresh anxieties from within the Organization and without, none of which helps our diplomatic efforts. There are still other times when governments choose not to be involved or when the UN as a body cannot act and the secretary-general must assume responsibility alone. Whether he likes it or not, his efforts will be approved by some and violently criticized by others. As U Thant noted:

> [I]n any serious situation, the actions of the Secretary General are naturally considered by some governments to be too strong, and by others to be too weak. ... There is often a wide gap between what some people wish he would do – or not do – and what others, including the public, expect of him.

This inventory may seem long, but it is very real, and I have recited it to indicate that the solutions we achieve come hard. Little can be realized without the willingness of the member states involved.

The need to maintain impartiality does not give me much free rein to express my own personal views or reactions openly, a safety valve most individuals use to alleviate stress and fatigue or to work out thorny situations. For that reason I count myself lucky to be able to discuss the problems I face with my wife. Elisabeth – or Cissy, as we call her – is trained in law and very much attuned to the nature of my work. She brings to UN issues a deep concern, tempered by a clarity of intellect, that makes her an ideal partner for candid discussions whenever I am weighing pros and cons. Her ability to wrest encouragement from setbacks is uncanny and most therapeutic, though I tend to be more patient of my critics than does she. Many diplomats might do well to heed Truman's pithy advice: 'If you can't stand the heat, stay out of the kitchen.' But long years of public service have conditioned me to political and diplomatic heat and, frankly, I don't mind it.

For all its pressures and frustrations, the job of being spokesman for an international organization wherein a majority of newly independent states are free to lodge their rightful claim to a better existence is uniquely challenging. To people who complain that in the United Nations there is too much talk and too little action, I can only say, as one who went through World War II and the deprivations of its aftermath, that verbal battle in the conference halls is preferable by far to military combat. That the United Nations has remained a constructive, working instrument for peace until today is, in itself, a triumph of international collaboration. To help preserve it, to enhance its usefulness, to husband its achievements and to realize its goals I consider both a privilege and an obligation.

CHAPTER TWO

Coming of Age

THE TWO EXTERNAL FORCES that most shape a man and determine the direction he will take are generally held to be the precepts of those who nurture him in childhood and the cultural impact of the society in which he grows. I gratefully acknowledge that the values, attitudes, and example I received from my parents and elders would have benefited me in any honourable pursuit I might have wished to undertake. But, looking back, I am convinced that the greatest impetus to my choosing a diplomatic and political career was provided by the circumstances and events of the era in which I grew to manhood.

I was born in 1918, scarcely a month after the armistice that marked the end of World War I and the collapse of the Austro-Hungarian Empire had been signed. World War II broke out the year I came of age. In the two intervening decades – those twenty youthful years that leave their stamp on a man – my Austria was an infant republic in search of equilibrium, and I was part and parcel of a people groping for identity amid the social disarray brought on by economic and political upheaval.

The impact of my country's desperate condition was inescapable during those years. Every Austrian felt the demoralizing effects of party rivalries and power plays, abortive insurrections, repression of subversive activity, the civil strife of 1934, the murder of Chancellor Dollfuss that same year by Nazi agents, and, finally, the fateful *anschluss*. World War I had drained Austria. Set adrift, its mighty parent dead, its expectations crushed, the new republic could not sustain itself. Deprived of raw materials and commodities previously available from other regions of the empire, its industries languished and its agricultural output fell to disastrously low levels. Every basic necessity was in short supply.

Against that background my family, like most of Austria, endured a harsh day-to-day existence. We lived in St Andrae-Woerdern with my maternal grandparents. They had been people of comfortable means before the war, but a heart attack in 1917 had forced my grandfather to give up farming and sell his land. Inflation and the subsequent devaluation reduced his post-war income to a pittance. The *krone* dropped to a fraction of its former value, stocks plummeted, and my family, along with so many others of the middle class, found itself poverty-stricken, often near starvation. There was no United Nations then to help us.

My mother, good countrywoman that she was, tried to keep up our morale, enveloping us all in the security of her affection. It was from my father that I learned to love my studies. He was a teacher and, later, the district school inspector for Tulln. He regarded nothing more important than the proper education of his three children and willingly did without to meet our school expenses. My brother Walter, who died in 1973, chose to follow in his footsteps and enjoyed a satisfying career in teaching. My sister Linde proved to have a scientific bent and is now chief of radiology in a hospital near Vienna. I would hope that in our respective ways we three have justified the sacrifices both our parents made.

The little town of Tulln, to which we had moved when my father was appointed school inspector, had no secondary school. The nearest *gymnasium* was thirty kilometres away. Regardless of the weather, I had to rouse myself from bed at five o'clock each morning, catch the train at six, ride for three quarters of an hour, and then trudge another half an hour to get there. I ate my breakfast on the way, usually a sandwich that my mother made for me from whatever little was available.

Between the station and the school there was a pastry shop. Its window display drew me like a magnet. It was my daily ritual to stop in front of that glass and covet every cake, tart and biscuit. I was always hungry. Most of Austria was always hungry. One day, while I was making my vicarious selection, an old friend of my father's greeted me and, after the usual exchange of courtesies, invited me to choose any sweet I wished. My hesitation was short-lived, and my dilemma such that I came away with several. I shall remember that treat all my life.

In retrospect, my early years at the *gymnasium* seem uneventful. The weeks and months were mostly taken up with trekking back and forth and with lessons, games, parental reprimands, and academic exhortations, not to mention the indiscriminate consumption of practically anything digestible, the transient joys and desperation, the chatter, pranks, and peccadilloes that normally engage the energy and curiosity of boys that age. It was not until my fifteenth year that politics assumed any significance. I was aware, of course, that my father was an avowed Christian Socialist, that he attended public meetings at which he sometimes was the speaker, and that he enjoyed considerable status in the district because of his involvement in community affairs. Political and social issues had always figured in the conversation of my parents and their friends, and, from time to time, I was sufficiently intrigued by what was said to ask for an explanation. I even drew upon this imperfect knowledge to speak with unwarranted authority among my own companions whenever, by chance, the opportunity arose. But until my fifteenth year, though I'd had long, direct experience of our country's economic ills, I had not yet awakened to its political afflictions.

In 1933, the enormity of what was happening suddenly shocked me and my companions out of boyhood. Our adolescent bickering became bitter quarrelling as partisan antagonisms intensified. Friendships broke on party lines – National Socialist, Social Democrat, or Christian Socialist. As parliamentary order fell apart and government by decree took over, it was clear that Austria was being pushed to a crisis. The situation required more sophisticated reasoning than I could muster, but I felt compelled, for my own satisfaction, to probe the interplay of national and international developments and to try to analyse the implications and the consequences.

In 1934, civil war broke out between the Christian Socialists and the Social Democrats. It sickened me to see men sprawled in the streets and know that the wetness on the pavement was their blood. I was confused and horrified. I told my father that I could not understand the passions that drove Austrians to kill each other. True, the Social Democrats were a radical element espousing what they themselves called Austro-Marxism. I knew, however, that when they were in power just after the war, their social programmes had been good and of benefit to the working class. The issues on which the parties disagreed did not seem to me to justify such slaughter, such destruction. From what I saw and heard I sensed the coming danger. The events that followed in quick order supported my misgivings. The schism gave Nazi enterprise a clear advantage and, within a short time, Austrian sovereignty had been usurped. Conservative and Socialist leaders who opposed annexation were soon to find themselves in the same concentration camps, with time to ponder the futility of their dispute and, in the face of common disillusion, reconcile their differences of ideology.

I finished my secondary schooling in 1936, the year the government instituted compulsory military service. Though I hadn't yet reached the required age, my family and I thought it best for me to sign up right away so that I might afterwards pursue my studies without interruption. Since I liked horses, I chose the cavalry for my one-year stint.

Returning to civilian life the following year, I began my law studies at the university and, at the same time, registered at the Vienna Consular Academy. The admission fees at the Academy were high. My father agreed to the necessary outlay, although he would have preferred my studying medicine. His support was all the more to be appreciated because I knew that the opportunities in the field I had chosen were far fewer than those in medicine. Unemployment was widespread and the prospects for law graduates were dim. Many young professionals quit the country altogether and went to Germany or, if they could afford the passage, to America.

Despite the affection and respect that I felt for my father, I had already begun to exercise a certain intellectual independence, which he was the first to encourage. He was strong in his convictions and concerned that I should be so in mine, whatever these might be. One issue on which we disagreed was political affiliation. Where he was active in the Christian Socialist party, I remained aloof. I could never bring myself to give allegiance wholly to any single party, since I was already convinced that I could better serve the interests of my country by staying free of partisan obligation. Even in the presidential election of 1971, although the People's party (post-war successor to the old Christian Socialists) endorsed my candidature, I stood as an independent and stressed that position in my campaigning.

Similarly, I have always held that religion must remain separate from politics. In our family, faith was perceived as a deeply personal commitment that must derive from individual volition. A priest at school had already taken great pains to teach me that religion has more to do with love and humanitarian concern than creed and that all great faiths embody principles akin to the Ten Commandments so fundamental to my own Catholic convictions. Those early lessons have been greatly reinforced by my experiences in the diplomatic service. I have met many peoples and learned much of many cultures other than my own, and these encounters have only expanded my religious outlook. That is why I maintain that the spiritual aspirations of all peoples and all religions must be respected quite apart from other human enterprise, since they are universally directed towards improving our common condition.

Today, regardless of political or ecclesiastical persuasion, Austrians entertain a passionate attachment to the democratic process as the only system of government whereby individual freedom and social progress can be assured. The concept of proletarian dictatorship no longer enjoys currency among the Socialists, and the party has come to operate for truly social democratic change within the framework of the national constitution. The Conservatives – if such they can be called these days – mindful of the grim consequences of their 1933 proscription of the Social Democratic party, eschewed authoritarianism and religious bias and in 1945 regrouped to form the People's party. At present one may find adherents of the Catholic faith among the Socialists, and certain Populists who profess agnosticism. This harmony and accommodation did not come about, however, until the world had undergone six years of global anguish and, starting even earlier, Austria had suffered the ignominious paralysis of Nazi annexation and then begun its long, slow convalescence under Allied occupation.

On 12 March 1938, the German army, in an awesome show of strength, marched into Austria. Reunification with the German Reich was formally proclaimed the following day. On 14 March, Hitler arrived in Vienna. Newsreel footage of the occasion gives evidence of a tumultuous welcome by the Viennese. Not one journalist or photographer ventured from the scene of celebration to less conspicuous corners of the capital to film the thousands sitting soberly at home. No camera caught the panic-stricken desperation of thousands more hiding in the city's cellars fearing the persecutions that were to begin at once.

My father was arrested a few days after annexation. I came home one evening from the university to find that the Gestapo had taken him away without a word. It wasn't hard to guess their reasons, but what they planned to do became a nightmare of anxiety. My father was known to be a loyal patriot who openly and publicly defended Austrian independence. Immediately the

German juggernaut was in position, he had been denounced by local Nazi sympathizers. Nothing he had said or done justified the punitive attitude of the new authorities. Still, he was made to feel the pressure of their intimidation and vindictive tactics, for, although he was released on sufferance, they forced him to resign immediately and deprived him of all normal means of livelihood.

We were almost penniless. Walter, Linde, and I continued with our studies none the less. An aunt and a group of friends pooled whatever they could spare to help us. I met my academic fees by tutoring and managed to continue at the Consular Academy in the morning and at the university in the afternoon and evening. I was still getting up at five to make the trip from Tulln to Vienna, and was having my own troubles with the police, who made a point of often stopping me and challenging my movements. Curiously enough, those interrogations lessened as the year went on, probably because they knew that I was about to be drafted.

It was impossible to escape military service. There were some, of course, with bureaucratic influence, sufficient money and relatives abroad who were able to secure an exit visa by paying the required fees, and doubtless a little more. But even a visa was no guarantee that one would be allowed to leave the country, since all such requests were subject to approval by the Germans. Otherwise, able-bodied Austrians of military age had little choice.

I was called up, along with my brother, just as World War II began. Since Walter and I were reservists, our only alternative was a court-martial. Actually, at that period, a soldier was better off than a civilian if his politics were questionable. Our family was under constant police surveillance. My father was detained from time to time, we were always being questioned, and I lived in daily fear. In the army there was less harassment of those known to disapprove of Nazism. In fact, it rather surprised me, especially in the light of what was going on at home, but vigilance was so relaxed that a number of the officers in my unit freely criticized the Nazi system with no great worry over the risk. As I got to know them, I suspected that a few were even engaged in underground activity. Later on, in 1944, I was not at all surprised to learn that army officers had been implicated in the 20 July assassination plot that marked a turning point in Hitler's fortunes. The fact that there were so many more anti-Nazis in the army than in the civil service probably had a lot to do with the relative permissiveness. Though we always had to exercise discretion, at least our disaffection was allowed more scope. Anti-Nazi literature was circulated under cover, and, of course, I read it all. I found men who shared my views, and our long discussions gave us a chance to air our feelings. Sunday mass was always well attended. It provided us with a rallying point and a means of manifesting our opposition to the notoriously anti-religious policies of the régime. Even so, the knowledge that I was serving in the German army was hard to bear. Deliverance from my bitter situation finally came when our unit moved into active combat on the Eastern front in 1941. I was wounded in the leg and medically discharged.

By the time I was repatriated in 1942, it had become impossible to leave the country. The borders had been closed and were being heavily patrolled. Everywhere the most ordinary movement was restricted, and the authorities dealt arbitrarily with anyone who did not conform to the regulations. I was permitted to resume my studies towards a doctorate in law, which I obtained some two years later. The preparation of my dissertation, dealing with the federalist principles of the German diplomat Konstantin Frantz, was not made any easier by the fact that the university library had been dispersed because of the bombings and the books and documents that I needed had been hidden in obscure and often widely scattered sites. I had to go from place to place and dig the information out in bits and pieces. Under other circumstances, the detective work involved might have been enjoyable. As it was, between the police, suspicious of my civilian status, and the bureaucrats, suspicious of my motives, the physical assembly of my source material turned out to be more exhausting than the research and the writing.

It was during this period that I became acquainted with Elisabeth, who was also studying law. We met for the first time at a conference at the university in 1943. She was twenty-two and I twenty-six when we were married a year later in August 1944. We had planned to spend our honeymoon in a little mountain village not far from Vienna, but our train had hardly cleared the city when the air-raid warning sounded. We were hustled off and spent our wedding night in the crowded basement of a local railway station, listening to the bombs falling overhead. The war was in its final year and the bombardment of Vienna was relentless. As the year drew to a close, the fighting so intensified that Elisabeth sought refuge in the countryside of Styria to await our first child, Liselotte. She was born the following May, a few weeks after Austria's liberation by the Allied forces. I remember thinking that her coming on the heels of a terrible war was a repetition of my own beginning, and I prayed that out of its long agony and immediate desolation the world might fashion an abiding peace so that she and children everywhere might never suffer such adversity.

Four months after Liselotte was born we moved to Baden. My parents were living there by then. Their persecution by the authorities and Nazi vandals had driven them from Tulln. At least the family would be together while I tried to find employment. My father, with his customary generosity, had offered to provide for us until I had a job.

The move itself was punishing. We made the journey in a cattle car chock-a-block with produce, poultry, freight of every kind, and as many other passengers as could be squeezed aboard. We were crammed against the baby's cradle, and her carriage sat atop the trunks and baggage that held everything we owned. Elisabeth, who was not well, rested on a pile of straw. I held my own perched on an apple crate. Every now and then she and I exchanged places to keep our limbs from getting cramp; but we didn't dare give up our places by the baby. It was impossible to sleep and there was certainly no room to stretch our legs. Any absolutely necessary move meant shifting things about and provoked glares and grumblings of resentment from the others.

The trip, which ordinarily took three hours, lasted two-and-a-half days. Control along the line of demarcation between the Russian and American zones of occupation was scrupulously observed. We stopped for hours at indeterminable places and innumerable little stations, whose names we couldn't even ascertain because our cattle car had no windows, and they seldom let us leave the train. We were hungry and, above all, thirsty. Liselotte never stopped crying. By the third and final night all the passengers were showing signs of strain. One of them, vexed beyond endurance, threatened to smash the baby's cradle to give himself more room. No move that we've made since, no matter where my assignments took us, has ever equalled that ordeal.

The pleasure of reunion when we finally reached Baden was somewhat dimmed by the conditions that awaited us. My parents' house had been bombed, and the windows in the part we were to occupy had all been blown out. Though we blocked them up as best we could, we nearly froze to death that winter. Fuel was hard to come by, and material for repairs non-existent. Finding enough to eat, however, proved our biggest problem. The only way we managed was to walk far into the countryside and go from farm to farm asking for any surplus they might have for sale.

In November 1945, the Austrian Ministry of Foreign Affairs offered me a post. For me, it wasn't just a job, it was *the* job – the one I wanted more than any other. I had passed the stiff competitive examination. Of the dozen candidates considered, only four of us had been accepted. It was a very modest post, but it was in the Ministry. All my academic preparation, all my interests, all my hopes had been geared to diplomatic service. At that moment, I felt content.

CHAPTER THREE

From Diplomacy to Politics

When I first reported to the Ministry on the Ballhausplatz I was twenty-six-years old, a family man and earnest in my plans. I came with all the formal requisites that might reasonably be expected of a fledgling diplomat. But, in addition, I brought with me a long-standing dream born of experience and sustained by hope. Heart and soul, I wanted to help create a world in which oppression and injustice, greed, hostility and confrontation and all the corresponding social ills would not be tolerated, one in which my country might regain an honourable place and play a useful role. The decline of Austria, the collapse of Europe and the wretchedness of war were deeply etched into my consciousness. I knew what hunger and privation were and what it meant to lose one's national identity and have to bend to foreign masters. At the same time, I recognized that there were rights and conditions to which people everywhere aspired, and I believed wholeheartedly that they could be attained. I was determined to lend whatever talents I possessed to that endeavour.

From 1945 to 1948 I remained in Vienna, at first carrying out the usual humble tasks entrusted to a novice. After a few months, however, I became secretary to Austria's first post-war foreign minister, Karl Grubner, and thus had ample opportunity to observe his working methods and how he dealt with international issues. It was a very valuable apprenticeship for me, because the occupation of the country by the Allied powers posed almost insurmountable problems for Austria in its efforts to achieve full independence.

In order to be near the Ministry that first year, I boarded in a modest room close by and went back to Baden only on weekends. But the trip was arduous, involving uncertain transportation and a three-hour walk at the Baden end. Both Cissy and I found the separation increasingly difficult, so in 1946 we took a small apartment in Vienna. We have always thought of that as the real beginning of our diplomatic life.

I longed to go abroad, to see at first hand the people and places that I had only read about in books. I had never really travelled anywhere except the areas surrounding home. Until 1918, Vienna had been the capital of a huge empire comprised of many countries. This was reflected in the ethnic diversity of its population. It had been a thriving European centre. Despite the depredation, traces of its former cosmopolitan importance were still visible and aroused in me a curiosity to know what lay beyond.

My first foreign assignment came in 1948, when I was posted to our embassy in Paris. That provided useful training, for we operated on a shoestring budget, and each member of our very limited staff carried a full and varied workload. As first secretary of the legation, I often had to serve as *chargé d'affaires* when the ambassador was away. In 1951, I was returned to Vienna as head of the Ministry's department of personnel, a post I held until 1955, the year the Allied occupation ended. My first direct encounter with the United Nations came that spring, when I was appointed permanent observer to the United Nations in New York. On 14 December 1955, I witnessed the admission of my country to full membership in the Organization.

For the next four years I served in Canada, first as minister and, later, as ambassador. In 1960, I went back to Vienna to head the Western branch of the Ministry's Political Department for the next two years and then was made director-general of political affairs until, in 1964, I returned to the United Nations as permanent representative of Austria. In January 1968, my government called me home again to offer me the post of federal minister for foreign affairs, an honour I accepted with the feeling that I'd reached the peak of my career.

In those twenty-three years of service I had seen the diplomatic role undergo dramatic changes and foreign policy assume new meanings, in part because of the special problems of the post-war period, but principally because of the development of democratic forms of government and the increasing influence of the media in forming public opinion. The modern diplomat must be prepared to deal publicly, often extemporaneously, with matters far beyond the scope of politics. He is expected to be informed on a wide variety of economic, social, legal and scientific issues and be ready to set forth his government's views on all of these. International co-operation these days frequently requires the diplomat to work on problems that are by no means strictly political. He may find himself obliged to deal with questions of agricultural development, customs tariffs, shipping, copyright, space research, ecology, or labour legislation. For that reason alone he must familiarize himself with a formidable range of subjects. When I served as chairman of the United Nations outer space committee, I had to do a heavy job of homework on that esoteric subject. Those of us on the committee who weren't specialists read scores of books and documents so that we might better understand the aspects that concerned us. That same intensive study was again necessary when I was appointed chairman of the safeguards committee of the International Atomic Energy Agency. In these complex times, the diplomat must be a fairly nimble-minded generalist able to turn his intellect and skills to almost any kind of problem.

As every experienced foreign service officer knows, personal feelings have no place in international diplomacy. Just as a government cannot be guided by emotions in protecting its interests, so the diplomat cannot allow his own personal bias to affect his purpose. If he is to be successful, he must base his attitude on the rational assessment of facts and forces, since concessions generally stem not from generosity but from the recognition of their inevitability. Agreement, after all, is nothing but a balance struck between opposing camps, a compromise between divergent interests. Good personal relations between diplomats can ease the process of negotiations, but the national interest takes precedence over respect or friendship, even over bonds of blood or culture, as history clearly shows.

Another factor that has become important in recent years is the growth of active public interest in governmental affairs. The diplomat now must take into account the susceptibilities and wishes of the people, for these are given wide dissemination by the media and greatly influence a country's politics. The outcome of diplomatic negotiation often depends as much on the political interplay of internal forces as on external circumstances.

Austrian independence is a case in point. The treaty of 15 May 1955, formally establishing my country as a sovereign, independent, and democratic state, would never have been achieved if all the political forces involved had not worked together. After ratification and the deposit of the ratification documents, the Austrian state treaty came into force on 27 June 1955. On that same day, the Allied Council in Vienna was dissolved. On 25 October, the last of the occupation armies left. The next day, the Austrian National Assembly passed the federal constitutional law on permanent neutrality.

Those events were significant in three ways. In the first place, after years of confrontation, East and West had agreed to relinquish their respective zones of occupation. Second, Austrian diplomacy had found a formula that gave the country a universally acceptable role in post-war Europe. Finally, the Soviet policy of *détente* begun by Nikita Khrushchev created a favourable climate for realization of the Austrian concept.

Khrushchev, whose joviality masked the seriousness of his efforts to achieve *détente* admired the enormous technological progress of the West and recognized its importance. He considered it in the Soviet Union's interest to restore trust among the Allies and to bring about peaceful co-existence. His attitude left little doubt of his conviction that a policy of *détente* would allow for the peaceful solution of many of the problems existing between states of different ideologies. Possibly he hoped that Austria would serve as an example.

The Austrian example, however, has not been followed, perhaps because, in a large measure, circumstances and geopolitical considerations applicable only to Austria dictated the solution finally arrived at. For Austria, of course, its state treaty and status of neutrality have proved a blessing. It is a healthy country now, and the reputation it enjoys clearly demonstrates that a small state can be a constructive factor in the normalization of international relations and the balance of power.

Austria's neutrality does not extend to ideology. My country is committed to Western democratic principles, and it is sometimes difficult to reconcile its neutrality with internal ideological freedom. I experienced this difficulty in 1968 when I was foreign minister and events in Czechoslovakia brought on a serious international crisis that, fortunately, proved short-lived. The events of August 1968 are understandable only if one accepts the fundamental fact that central Europe is a zone in which East-West interests clash. I felt that the Czechoslovakian crisis would not precipitate a military confrontation, that the superpowers, mindful of the realities of the Yalta Agreement, would want to avoid full-scale conflict. Thankfully, I was right in my assessment; but at the time I could not be sure that my countrymen fully understood the situation or its implications *vis-à-vis* our foreign policy. Many Austrians were still adapting to the new conditions arising from neutrality. In *The Austrian Example*, which I wrote in 1970, I emphasized the factors that had so long inhibited its independence, so that Austrians, in particular, might better understand the delicate but viable relationship between their country's internal democratic structure and its foreign policy.

There is no question that my countrymen are keenly interested in politics, both national and international. I saw that clearly when campaigning for the federal presidency in 1971, during which I met with Austrians from all walks of life in every region of the country. I was especially struck by the political awareness of the young, by their readiness and ability to look beyond immediate domestic problems and grasp the broader implications of world issues. I did not win the election, but I gained much insight into the attitudes of people, as well as into the importance of the media and the inner workings of politics.

The knowledge thus acquired, combined with my experience as a diplomat and my nationality, was surely an asset in my becoming secretary-general. Since the United Nations operates on democratic parliamentary principles, there are two major considerations in the selection of a candidate for that high office. The first concerns the impartiality of the candidate and his country and the adherence of both to the principles of the United Nations Charter. The second, of course, concerns the candidate's personal ability, his knowledge of the correlations of world politics and his understanding of the expectations of the new and smaller states, as well as those of the established countries. Evidently, the member states were satisfied that I met these criteria when they elected me in 1971 and re-elected me in 1976.

Austria, indeed, has a high regard for the United Nations and its Charter. Between the two wars it suffered directly the disastrous consequences of the failure of the League of Nations. Made up mainly of European states, the League, at best, served as a complement to bilateral diplomacy. Many felt that its impotence to establish and maintain a genuine international order helped foster Hitler's opportunist policies. Austrians are very conscious of the differences between the United Nations and its predecessor. Those of my generation gratefully remember the United Nations Relief and Rehabilitation Administration teams that shortly after liberation in 1945 distributed free milk and other basic foodstuffs to our undernourished children, including my own Liselotte. That positive response to our nation's needs did much to stimulate a general wish among Austrians to belong to the world body although, until the signing of the state treaty, Austria had to be content with participating in the specialized agencies. Since its admission as a member state, however, it has gradually been included in all undertakings of international co-operation.

United Nations membership has bolstered Austria's security. In turn, the recognition of Austria's strict adherence to neutrality has been a stabilizing influence in central Europe. It is no coincidence, then, that Vienna has become a centre of United Nations activity. For some years now it has been the seat of the International Atomic Energy Agency and the United Nations Industrial Development Organization. A vast new complex on the Danube will soon house other UN institutions and secretariat units also serving the cause of world peace.

CHAPTER FOUR

A Mirror of the World

IS THE PUBLIC really justified in complaining, as it sometimes does, that the United Nations has accomplished nothing – that all it does is talk? I don't think so. The United Nations is certainly not above reproach, but those aspects of its operation most evident to the public sometimes obscure its real value. With two thirds of its membership consisting of less-developed countries, most of which have only recently gained independence, there is no question that the composition of the Organization has changed considerably since its foundation. There has been a decided shift in its activities towards questions of development and economics. In the face of growing interdependence, no government today is unaware that a new economic order is in the making and that a correct middle path must be found to accommodate the different political and ideological orientations. And yet there is much public feeling, especially in the West, that the United Nations should still continue to function as it did at the time of its creation and in the years preceding the great wave of decolonization of the last two decades. The average individual ignores the fact that UN membership has tripled since that time. He also fails to understand that the basic democratic structure and procedures of the Organization have remained the same and that the very principles and purposes which he espouses for his country must be operative for all. There is also a tendency to forget that the United Nations, by reason of its present universal composition, provides a central meeting place for almost all the countries of the world. In its conference halls, committee rooms and corridors, delegates can get to know each other. Many times behind the scenes, they find the opportunity to negotiate or even settle conflicts never aired publicly. The United Nations serves, moreover, as a platform for peoples who otherwise would have no means of being heard. These quiet, beneficial advantages – which, in reality, affect the lives of millions – are generally overlooked, while the flood of rhetoric and unavoidable reiteration that marks UN political debate is widely publicized.

The administrative and financial problems of the United Nations constitute another aspect of its operation that is often misunderstood. A detailed analysis of how UN activities are organized, co-ordinated, financed, and serviced would be inappropriate here, but some of the difficulties that arise for the secretary-general as chief administrative officer merit explanation. Many of these stem from the fact that the United Nations is primarily a political organization and, consequently, there are political overtones to all its operations, even straightforward budgetary matters that would be simple to administer under other circumstances. As it is, no member state can be compelled to pay its contribution to the regular budget, although its voting right may be suspended under the Charter if it falls behind for more than two years. Voluntary contributions to finance the numerous extra-budgetary programmes depend entirely on the generosity with which each state responds to the secretary-general's appeal. It does not matter that a programme has been approved by the majority and mandated by resolution. A state that does not wish to pay cannot be made to pay. The nations that do contribute recognize that there are many advantages to multilateral programmes under UN auspices, especially in maintaining good relations between the industrialized countries and the Third World. There are some countries, however, that are not happy with the anonymity of collective action and, for political reasons, prefer bilateral collaboration. This reduces the amount of money the United Nations has available for its operation or renders it uncertain. The consequence is that we are always operating under financial stringency.

Since taking office in 1972, I have consistently made every effort to extricate the Organization from its financial straits. We have limited expenditures as much as possible and have done our utmost to ensure the optimum rational use of our resources. But economies cannot be made at the expense of political and humanitarian objectives. The withdrawal of our peace-keeping forces from any of the areas in which they are operating, for example, might well invite a renewal of hostilities. And which of us would want to cut off aid to peoples victimized by man-made or natural disasters?

Budgetary limitations also affect the administration of the Secretariat, although certain of its shortcomings can be attributed to the Organization's growth, the recruitment stipulations of the Charter and the General Assembly, and the rivalries of member states. Contrary to a widely held belief, United Nations employees are not overpaid. The salaries that member states pay their diplomats are generally much higher than those we pay to our people, the majority of whom do not enjoy any diplomatic privileges whatsoever. Nor are they tax exempt. It says a great deal for his idealism if a highly qualified individual acepts a UN post, because his remuneration and conditions of employment would be far more advantageous in industry or elsewhere.

The nationality quotas that have been established also hamper our recruitment efforts. At the same time that we must ensure equitable geographical representation, we must base our selection of personnel on the highest standards of efficiency, competence and integrity – and sometimes it is difficult to find candidates who satisfy both these conditions. The member states watch appointments carefully, especially those for the higher posts, to see that they are fairly represented, and they sometimes exert considerable pressure to secure key positions for their own nationals.

Over the years, the Secretariat has instituted many measures to make its operation cost effective, and new waves are constantly being sought. Among other things, posts that fall vacant through retirement are filled only as the need arises. The efficiency of the Organization can sometimes be impaired by false economy, however. We are being asked to take on an increasing number of complex international responsibilities, yet we are not always given the best means for carrying out those mandates. It would be extremely practical, for instance, if the United Nations had permanent delegates accredited to the individual member states. That way we would be able to establish contact faster and more directly. But thus far that has not been feasible.

It would be wrong, I feel, to explain our short-comings solely on the basis of fiscal and administrative handicaps or to blame the other intramural factors that I have touched on. One should realize that the United Nations is, after all, the world in microcosm. Its weaknesses must consequently be ascribed primarily to the contradictions that characterize the world community itself.

One of the major problems to create great difficulties for many years was the Cold War. The superpowers now understand that there is no alternative to peaceful co-existence and they tend to intervene indirectly in zones where they have interests. They also show much greater flexibility than formerly in situations unfavourable to their interests. Still, this does not alter the fact that the rivalry between them remains a very real, very influential factor in world politics.

Bilateral or regional conflicts are unavoidable, and there are situations where they can endanger peaceful co-existence. The containment of such conflicts is one of the most important functions of the United Nations. The Helsinki conference on security and co-operation in Europe was a demonstration of the joint will to intensify collaboration. I am well aware of the grave reservations, even disappointment, felt in many circles concerning the practical results of that conference – and, even more so, the one in Belgrade. Neither fulfilled the hopes invested in them; nevertheless, they did represent an important effort to make progress.

The ability of the United Nations to contribute to world peace is a function of its universal character. That is why I always favoured the admission of the People's Republic of China to UN membership. It seemed to me absurd to strive for peace and world-wide concord without the participation of the largest nation on earth.

The Chinese are an industrious and proud people, anxious to resume their rightful place in world affairs and learn more of Western technology. As carefully as they guard their own independence, they respect the independence of others. They have given aid to Third World countries, constructing roads in Yemen or building railways in Zambia and Tanzania. But when such projects are completed, they withdraw. The Chinese delegation to the United Nations is equally reticent. Its members will participate in the work of the General Assembly and the various commissions only – and they themselves have stressed this – if they believe themselves able to make a valid contribution. As a permanent member of the Security Council, China has seldom used its power of veto, even when it has not agreed with the methods proposed for dealing with a situation. In principle, it does not approve of United Nations peace-keeping operations. Nevertheless, in the Security Council, it did not oppose renewal of the mandate for the stationing of UN troops along the cease-fire lines in the Middle East. And, in the case of Cyprus, it has refrained from hindering the intercommunal discussions that have taken place under my aegis. On the other hand, the Chinese government actively supports UN efforts aimed at establishing a new world economic order and UN aid to less-developed countries.

Our task is not made any easier by the differences between China and the USSR and those between the latter and the United States. Amid these tensions, it is difficult to manoeuvre in the cause of peace. What seems acceptable to one is often rejected by the other. Misunderstandings abound and reproaches are forthcoming. The latter assume different forms, according to their origin.

Some are publicly pronounced, others more discreetly lodged. I have not always managed to prove such reproaches groundless, but I believe that my partners in discussion are convinced of my impartiality and good will.

In addition, the so-called North-South divergence between the industrialized and the less-developed countries has assumed more and more importance of late. Many less-developed nations do not consider the right of veto of the five permanent members of the Security Council to be justified, arguing that it was conferred solely on the basis of its holders' military and financial strength. In truth, more than half the normal budget of the United Nations is financed by a small number of industrialized states. So, too, with most UN assistance programmes maintained by voluntary contribution. The system of apportionment that is in use seemed totally justified to the founders of the Organization in view of the widely varying financial resources of the member states, especially at the outset. Even now, the per capita annual income in many countries stands at less than $200, while in others it ranges from $2,500 to over $5,000. If the contributions of the member states were based only on their population figures, then a country like India would have to pay more than double the 25 per cent currently contributed by the United States – which, incidentally, represents less than a dollar a year for the individual American taxpayer.

The less-developed countries feel that financial strength should not be a source of inordinate political influence, pointing out that, in a democratic system, rich and poor are equal before the law, irrespective of the taxes they pay.

I agree that a better allocation of contributions is certainly desirable. It would also be desirable that all member states, large and small, enjoy the same rights. But it is difficult to perceive at the moment how the right of veto can be abolished. Such amendment of the Charter would require ratification by two thirds of the member states, including all five permanent members of the Security Council, some of which are categorically opposed to giving up a privilege that, in their view, is justified by their special responsibilities in world politics as stipulated in the Charter.

It is often said, in defence of the present system, that the right of veto is a counterbalance to the 'automatic majority' of the Third World countries in the General Assembly. The Third World delegates retort that majority decisions are an essential characteristic of democracy and that doubts concerning the democratic structure of the Assembly arose only after the Western powers had lost their automatic majority.

In reality, there is no such thing as an automatic majority. The voting records in the Assembly prove this. It is true the less-developed nations unite on economic issues affecting their future. And, not surprisingly, most vote together on a limited number of political proposals, especially those concerning southern Africa. But the records also show that their decisions are often determined by widely varying ideologies and interests. A splintering of their votes is evident whenever Third World countries have been in conflict, as in the case of the former Spanish Sahara, North and South Korea, Djibouti, and Vietnam. On such issues many less-developed member states are apt to vote with one or the other of the big powers. Despite assertions to the contrary, no monolithic bloc prevails.

The admitted prejudices of various groups among the membership encourage the tendency to sometimes by-pass the United Nations and regulate problems unilaterally or bilaterally. When they feel reason to distrust the outcome, the parties in conflict do not wish to risk arbitration by the Security Council or judgement by the General Assembly. An obvious instance was the Vietnam war. Despite the courageous negotiating efforts of U Thant, all parties rejected UN intervention. The Republic of North Vietnam and the Viet Cong were certain that the United States would exercise undue influence in the United Nations, while Washington feared the collective influence of the Third World countries.

Undiscouraged by the situation, in April 1972, I publicly

offered my good offices to help end the bloodshed. 'I shall need the support of the governments,' I said. 'If the governments concerned do not wish to claim my services, that is their affair; but they should not reproach the United Nations afterwards.' I then initiated intensive diplomatic contacts with all sides and proposed a compromise solution, the conclusion of which could be facilitated by the United Nations. Although I harboured no great hopes, I was convinced that sooner or later they would have to turn to us for multilateral help on certain problems.

Less than a year later, I was invited to attend the Paris Peace Conference as an observer. My presence there enabled me to bring the United Nations into the negotiations and to have some confidential discussions with the North Vietnamese delegation and with Madame Binh, then foreign minister of the provisional revolutionary government of South Vietnam. I felt that the time had come for us to establish relations, even if they were to be restricted to humanitarian undertakings. Madame Binh agreed. In the course of our discussions, she suggested, with tact and firmness, that her government be given the status of permanent observer to the United Nations.

The American government raised objections to the entry of Vietnamese observers into the United States, but eventually it was agreed to establish a liaison office in Geneva that would enable the UN High Commissioner of Refugees, UNICEF, and other UN agencies to furnish aid to the stricken people of Vietnam. When the fighting resumed, the American authorities asked me to use my relations with their adversaries to facilitate the carrying out of various humanitarian operations. Since the cessation of hostilities, millions in that war-torn country have benefited from our assistance.

The tenacity of the North Vietnamese and their southern allies, the weakness of the Saigon régime, and the intense unpopularity of the war in the United States were the principal factors in bringing that conflict to an end. The reunification of the Vietnam nation was the logical outcome of those circumstances.

Nationalism is an inevitability of our time that must be reckoned with. When it develops within the framework of international co-operation it is a force for good. It becomes negative only when it is set apart from the interests of the world community for purely selfish ends. On numerous occasions, the United Nations has demonstrated its ability to protect the national interests of all parties in a dispute, avoiding military confrontation and the complications that bilateral diplomacy sometimes produces. It would be sad, indeed, if our services were sought only when the prevention of irreparable harm becomes impossible.

The United Nations was created to deal with crises and will continue to fulfil its international responsibilities. At the same time, I should point out that it is no more than a mirror of the world it serves. That world is a conglomerate of extremely varied, often intractable, passionate, and antagonistic nations, each with its own character, geography, and history. If the United Nations pretended to be more than a true reflection of human society, its usefulness would wane. As Dag Hammarskjöld explained: 'We must accept the United Nations for what it is: an imperfect but indispensable instrument for realizing a juster and more secure world order by peaceful means.'

CHAPTER FIVE

Powers and Limitations of the United Nations

A FUNDAMENTAL RESPONSIBILITY of the United Nations, one in which the secretary-general is often directly involved, is the defence of human rights. But what the public does not fully understand is that in pursuing this delicate obligation, the secretary-general is hampered by the fact that he represents an organization of sovereign states bound by the provisions of the United Nations Charter. In the preamble of the Charter, the signatory states declare their faith 'in fundamental human rights, in the dignity and worth of the human person, in the equal rights of men and women'. Under Article 1, defining the purposes of the Organization, the UN membership is pledged 'to achieve international co-operation . . . in promoting and encouraging respect for human rights and for fundamental freedoms for all without distinction as to race, sex, language, or religion'. These provisions would appear to give the Organization and its secretary-general authority to intervene whenever human rights are violated. But the initiatives that we may undertake concerning human rights, as well as other matters, are clearly limited by Article 2, which states:

> Nothing contained in the present Charter shall authorize the United Nations to intervene in matters which are essentially within the domestic jurisdiction of any state or shall require the Members to submit such matters to settlement under the present Charter.

Our power to act is further restricted by other considerations. The international community has yet to arrive at a uniform definition of what constitutes a 'human rights' violation. Here the attitude of the different states is not determined by moral criteria alone. Governments tend to judge violations by friendly states leniently and to harshly condemn those by political opponents. There is also the ideological question of whether the civil and political rights of citizens should take precedence over their economic, social, and cultural rights. Some governments of newly-independent states, for example, consider it more important to feed and educate their people than to give them the vote, especially since the importance of the latter may not be fully understood by an illiterate electorate. Many states also believe that national development necessitates certain restrictions on the rights of the individual.

Critics often accuse the United Nations of lacking objectivity or staying power in upholding human rights. They forget that our involvement in such matters is determined by the intergovernmental organs, such as the Commission on Human Rights and the Economic and Social Council. The secretary-general has no right to lay down rules by which the world community should maintain its principles, although within his limitations he should do all he can to promote and facilitate progress towards the realization of the aims established by international conventions. Even with such limitations, he can still find considerable scope to exert influence.

My guideline in the defence of human rights is: the good of the people concerned. I offer my services unofficially, on a purely humanitarian basis. Whether it be a matter of intervening to unite families, protecting the rights of a national minority, or alleviating harsh sentences, I am always extremely careful to assure the government concerned that I do not intend to interfere in its internal jurisdiction. Because most governments are loath to be accused of succumbing to outside pressure, I often conduct my interventions without publicity. But I have never hesitated to make a public appeal if I believe the circumstances warrant it.

In view of the despair that still exists throughout the world, it is disillusioning to realize that our efforts to abolish injustice are constantly resisted and that the great ideals of the Organization often have to yield to practical political considerations. Still, the record proves that we have not failed altogether. Since the adoption of the Universal Declaration of Human Rights in December 1948, the principles that it sets forth have been incorporated into the constitutions of many new states and have unquestionably been a positive influence on international ethics. They form the basis of the international covenants on civil and political rights and on economic, cultural, and social rights that followed in 1966 and of the more modest, though important, declaration on torture adopted by the General Assembly in 1975. Our inability to score more rapid and substantial success in securing the universal enjoyment of human rights may be disappointing, but it only stiffens our determination.

A growing problem is international terrorism. In recent years, we have attempted to define this phenomenon and its causes in order to distinguish it sharply and impartially from national liberation activities – but opinions are still divided. In principle, of course, all terrorist activities are censurable. In reality, they are not always universally condemned, especially if they are actions that stem from the legitimate aspirations of a liberation movement. In deciding to place the problem of terrorism on the agenda of the General Assembly in 1972, in view of the steady rise in terrorist activity, I explained my initiative as follows:

> I consider it the duty of the General Assembly to examine this question and take appropriate measures to prevent any future acts of violence against innocent people. This question should be treated from a general point of view. . . . The situation is extraordinarily serious and worrying. . . . It is our duty to act.

A number of Third World nations feared that the international action against terrorism that I was requesting might serve to work against national liberation movements. In my statement to the General Committee of the Assembly, I tried to make it absolutely clear that my proposal in no way intended to obstruct the inalienable right of nations to fight for the achievement of their independence. At the same time I emphasized that it would be pointless to tackle the problem without examining its political causes and suggested that the question be submitted to the legal (sixth) committee of the Assembly for preliminary examination. Although an *ad hoc* committee on terrorism was established and continues to report to the legal committee, this item still remains on the agenda of the General Assembly because of differences of definition. Nevertheless, some convergence of views is perceptible. A number of states are coming to recognize that acts of terrorism only damage the political cause they claim to be serving. In December 1977, on the recommendation of its legal committee, the General Assembly adopted two resolutions, condemning international terrorism and calling for the drafting of a convention against the taking of hostages and for improved security measures against the hijacking of aircraft.

Unlike human rights and international terrorism, purely humanitarian assistance is the one activity that seldom provokes controversy in the United Nations. Here the entire membership responds with unaccustomed alacrity and accord. Probably the most successful massive aid programme in the history of the United Nations was that undertaken in the early 1970s for the new state of Bangladesh, where war, political unrest and floods had created additional hardships for an already afflicted population. Many governments and private organizations participated in the relief efforts, which were co-ordinated and carried out by UN officials. In response to my appeals, sorely needed contributions in cash and in kind amounting to more than $1.6 billion were raised. The superb organization of the entire action under UN auspices enabled us to see that the relief supplies were not diverted and did reach the people they were intended for. We were also instrumental in facilitating the exchange of prisoners and the care of refugees. I would also like to think that my talks with

Indira Gandhi, Bhutto, and Mujibur Rahman helped improve relations among India, Pakistan, and Bangladesh.

We are still actively engaged in a sustained programme of assistance to the hard-pressed peoples of Mauritania, Senegal, Mali, the Upper Volta, Chad, and Niger in West Africa. Years of recurrent drought have plagued this region, resulting in the total devastation of harvests and livestock, and in widespread famine. Since 1972, when it became evident that a catastrophe was developing, the United Nations and various specialized agencies, principally the Food and Agriculture Organization and the World Food Programme, have co-ordinated efforts to deal, first, with the immediate emergency and, in recent years, with the recovery and rehabilitation needs of the six hard-pressed countries.

Considering the United Nation's traditional response to crises, one might believe the major thrust of its activity more remedial than preventive. Actually, what has happened is that over the years the Organization has acquired the ability to mobilize and channel aid quickly and with maximum benefit. Because the media tend to headline only the emergency situations, UN humanitarian and peace-keeping involvement is well known. While such publicity is advantageous, it nevertheless overshadows the many quieter UN successes in preventing armed conflict. If one stops to think that most international differences contain the seeds for all-out war, then one should realize that settlement without resort to force is a contribution of the utmost importance. The United Nations has been able to forestall full-scale military conflict repeatedly. In 1974, for example, we played a significant role in defusing the tensions that had poisoned relations between Iran and Iraq for decades. The dispute was centred primarily on border delimitation and navigational rights in the Shatt-al-Arab estuary, although unrest among the Kurdish minority in Iraq was also a factor. There was every likelihood that the frequent border clashes would escalate into a major confrontation, which, as it turned out, both governments were anxious to avoid. My special representative, Luis Weckmann-Muñoz, was warmly received in Baghdad and Teheran. Through his efforts, an agreement was reached whereby both sides undertook the strict observance of a cease-fire and the withdrawal of troops along the entire frontier and an early resumption of conversations aimed at a comprehensive settlement of all bilateral issues was promised.

Because its duty is to prevent war, the United Nations has been intensifying its work towards disarmament, the attainment of which becomes increasingly urgent. As nuclear capability spreads the arms race accelerates and weaponry becomes more and more lethal, it is disquieting to realize that only modest progress has been made in disarmament negotiations both within and beyond the framework of the Organization. More than a hundred states have ratified the non-proliferation treaty; but several countries capable of producing nuclear weapons have not yet signed it and, consequently, are not bound by its provisions. The Antarctic treaty and the treaties banning nuclear weapons in outer space and under water have designated these uninhabited areas nuclear-weapon-free zones. To date, however, Latin America, under the 1967 treaty of Tlatelolco, is the only populated region on earth where nuclear weapons are proscribed, though the General Assembly has before it draft proposals to establish other nuclear-weapon-free zones elsewhere – in Africa and South Asia, for instance. Still, these treaties and initiatives are small successes in the struggle for disarmament, which, as I have stated repeatedly, is a struggle for the survival of mankind.

The arms race is accelerating alarmingly. Year after year, the statistics become more formidable. Annual global military expenditure has now reached a record $400 billion – a sum one thousand times greater than the total contributions of all the member states to the United Nations budget – and it continues to rise. Almost 6 per cent of the world's total output of goods and services is used for military purposes. The amount spent annually on military research and development is five times more than that spent on all other scientific research. Some 25 per cent of the world's scientific manpower is employed in armament-related projects, and the number of people serving the military complex (roughly sixty million) is equal to the entire industrial work-force of all Europe. It has been estimated that since the end of World War II military activities have consumed more than $6,000 billion, an amount equal to the combined gross national product of all the countries on earth in 1976. International trade in armaments has reached the unprecedented level of $20 billion annually, with most weapons going to the zones of conflict, particularly the Middle East, where an average of 16 per cent of the gross national product is allocated for the military.

These few statistics merely indicate the enormous spending generated by the arms race. Of the far more serious economic and social implications, a committee of experts which I appointed at the request of the General Assembly reported in 1977:

> The high level of military spending in the world not only diverts resources that are urgently needed for dealing effectively with economic development and growth problems but also helps to exacerbate these problems. Large military expenditures contribute to the depletion of natural resources, tend to aggravate inflationary tendencies, and add to existing balance-of-payments problems. In this way, they have contributed to economic disruption and political instability in some countries. Even so, the implications of an arms race and of military expenditures on the scale typical of the post-war period are much more pervasive than mere economic considerations would suggest. Being one of the main factors shaping the international context, the arms race exerts a profound influence on the politics, economy, and society of many countries. In some cases an ever present risk of interference by outside powers imposes narrow limits on foreign and domestic policies, limits that may run counter to national aspirations. In other cases the armed forces become a factor of decisive weight in international politics. Military priorities may also exert considerable influence on the directions taken by the civilian economy.

. . .

The most important feature of the arms race is that it undermines national, regional and international security. It involves the constant risk of war engaging the largest powers, including nuclear war, and it is accompanied by an endless series of wars at lower levels. It raises an ever greater barrier against the development of an atmosphere in which the role of force in international relations may be downgraded. In addition, it impedes relations between countries, affecting the volume and direction of exchanges, diminishing the role of co-operation among States, and obstructing efforts towards establishing a new international economic order on a more equitable basis.

So urgent has the problem become, and of such world-wide concern, that the General Assembly convened a five-week special session on disarmament in 1978 to formulate comprehensive guidelines whereby the complex business of concrete negotiation might be undertaken. The collective declaration of principles, the programme of action, and the establishment of improved machinery for direct negotiation under UN auspices that emerged from that session represent a vital step forward and should give new impetus to disarmament efforts.

CHAPTER SIX

Southern Africa

The United Nations has always supported the process of decolonization and encouraged those peoples under foreign domination who are striving for self-determination and independence. This policy corresponds to the provisions of the Charter and to the Declaration on the Granting of Independence to Colonial Countries and People, which was adopted by the General Assembly on 14 December 1960. In that Declaration, the Assembly demanded an end to colonialism in any form. At the same time, it stated that foreign domination or economic exploitation of any peoples constituted a denial of fundamental human rights, was contrary to the Charter, and formed an impediment to the promotion of world peace and co-operation. The General Assembly also declared that inadequate readiness of a people for independence, whether political, economic, social or educational, should never serve as a pretext for delaying the granting of independence. The unambiguous attitude of the United Nations in respect to decolonization has contributed considerably to the fact that since 1945 more than seventy states have achieved their independence and become members of the Organization.

The great era of decolonization, which began after World War II and is now almost ended, represents a remarkable phenomenon of our epoch. Usually the transition from colony to independent state was made without serious incident, although in a few cases the struggle for independence met with strong resistance by the colonial powers.

There are at present less than ten million people still living under colonial rule, mainly in southern Africa. The independence of the former Portuguese colonies has given new impetus to the efforts of the people of Zimbabwe (Southern Rhodesia) and Namibia (South West Africa) in their struggle for statehood.

From 1884, Namibia was under German administration until it was conquered by the South African army during World War I in 1915. After the armistice it was entrusted to South Africa as a mandated territory by the League of Nations. Under this mandate, South Africa was pledged to carry out a 'sacred trust of civilization' for the 'well-being and development' of the population of the territory that was to conclude with the granting of independence. Instead, the South African government introduced apartheid and, over the years, promulgated a sizable body of laws drastically restricting the rights of Africans. After World War II, it refused altogether to recognize the jurisdiction of the United Nations.

For thirty years, the United Nations tried to induce South Africa to fulfil its obligations. But despite patient negotiations and a great many resolutions and appeals, there has been, until now, little success in achieving independence for the territory.

On 27 October 1966, the General Assembly, by a vote of 114 to 2 (South Africa and Portugal), formally abolished South Africa's mandate over Namibia and placed the country under the direct authority of the United Nations. South Africa refused to comply with the resolution.

A dangerous situation had by this time developed within the country. Resistance increased; rebellious nationalists stepped up their activities; clashes became more frequent. The South African parliament, in 1967, adopted an anti-terrorism act, which, among other things, called for punishment by death or life imprisonment for certain activities.

Disregarding the resolutions of the General Assembly and the Security Council, the South African government, in 1969, transferred to the Republic most of the powers of the legislative assembly of Namibia. The United Nations regarded that as a further step towards annexation of the territory and declared all measures concerning Namibia taken by Pretoria since the repeal of the mandate to be null and void. On 30 January 1970, the Security Council issued an appeal to all states, particularly those with economic or other interests in the territory, to sever all relations with the South African government in so far as they involved Namibia.

Following an inquiry by the Security Council, on 21 June 1971, the International Court of Justice expressed the opinion that South Africa's administration of Namibia was illegal and that South Africa was under obligation to withdraw its administration from the territory immediately. The Court added that all UN member states should cease all contact with the South African government in so far as the latter was acting on Namibia's behalf.

In February 1972, the Security Council held a session in Africa for the first time in order to express its concern over the situation in Namibia. During that meeting, which was held in Addis Ababa, the Council requested me to meet with the parties concerned in pursuit of the goal specified by the Security Council: 'to enable the people of Namibia, freely and with strict regard to the principle of human equality, to exercise their right to self-determination and independence'.

In the spring of 1972 I travelled to South Africa and Namibia. In Capetown, I had a series of talks with the prime minister and the foreign minister, after which I visited various parts of Namibia and had an opportunity to meet with many of the local leaders. Later, I also talked with representatives of the Namibian liberation movement SWAPO (South West Africa People's Organization). The Security Council subsequently renewed my mandate twice, and I continued my efforts. Talks with those concerned were also conducted by my special envoy, the Swiss diplomat Albert Escher, who went to South Africa and Namibia in the autumn of 1972 before I resumed negotiations with South Africa's foreign minister in Geneva. To my great disappointment, our negotiations led nowhere. South Africa's leaders indicated that independence for Namibia might be possible in about ten years, a delay I considered unrealistic. In particular, no agreement could be reached on the decisive question of Namibia's territorial unity and abandonment of the Bantustan policy, i.e., partitioning the region into various semi-autonomous native states. My mission ended without success in December 1973.

In the light of those developments, the South African government decided to proceed on its own. It held a 'constitutional conference', the Turnhalle Conference, in Windhoek from 1975 to 1977. On the basis of a 'provisional constitution' elaborated during the conference, the territory was to be converted into a confederation of autonomous Bantustans that would be granted independence on 31 December 1978.

The United Nations decided that the Turnhalle Conference did not reflect the will of the population, in either its aims or its composition, inasmuch as some of the parties, notably SWAPO, had not participated. Only free elections held under United Nations supervision could give the country the structures of a modern state and so bring about genuine independence.

When South Africa announced its intention of realizing its own plans, the African states, together with other governments, again demanded the intervention of the Security Council and the employment of sanctions against South Africa under Chapter VII of the Charter. This led to the Security Council's unanimously adopting a resolution in January 1976 establishing the framework within which Namibia should attain independence under UN supervision and control. In an attempt to break the impasse, the five Western members of the Security Council undertook a joint initiative to achieve a universally acceptable solution on the basis of the prior resolutions of the Security Council. That initiative caused South Africa to announce, in June 1977, that it would forego carrying out the decisions of the Turnhalle Conference for the time being and await the result of the Western negotiation efforts.

In April 1978, the Western powers officially submitted to the Security Council their proposal for the carrying out of free elections throughout the territory that would permit the Namibians to determine the future of their country as a single political entity. It provided a detailed programme of action in which the United Nations would play a major role. Among other things, I was requested to appoint a special representative to supervise at all stages the measures taken for the preparation and carrying out of the elections and the orderly transition to full independence. The proposal also called for the dispatch of a sizable United Nations military component to guarantee peace and order until independence was achieved. Although some problems remained unsolved, among them the future of Walvis Bay, Namibia's only deep-sea port, the proposal represented a great step forward.

After intensive negotiations conducted by the five Western powers, the Security Council adopted a resolution in July 1978, requesting the secretary-general to submit a report containing his recommendations for the implementation of the Western plan in acordance with guidelines already approved by the Council. As is usually the case with such plans, many practical difficulties remained to be resolved, and there were certain gaps between the positions of the parties that had not been bridged. It was my task, with the help of my special representative for Namibia, Martti Ahtisaari of Finland, to try to bridge these gaps sufficiently for the United Nations operation in Namibia (the United Nations Transition Assistance Group) to establish itself in the territory and start on the programme of activities leading up to the supervised elections and the transition to full independence.

I was aware in advance that since there could be no perfect solution to so complex a situation, much would depend on the will of the parties concerned to make progress. In late August 1978, I submitted to the Security Council my report on the practical means for the implementation of the Western plan. This included a large civilian component and a military component some 7,500 strong. Even without the great political difficulties of the situation, the physical hardships and the size of the territory posed immense organizational and logistical problems for the United Nations.

My report, which, for the first time, made practical recommendations on the nature and the size of the United Nations operation, not surprisingly raised questions on both sides. South Africa, in particular, was bothered about the size of the military component; it also doubted that we would be able to secure a geographical composition of the component that could command its approval. SWAPO, for its part, had other reservations. It was thus impossible to embark on the operation immediately, as we had hoped, and a further period of negotiations and consultations ensued.

South Africa decided in the meantime to hold internal elections in the territory in December 1978 in defiance of strong UN objections. The elections, which were viewed by the United Nations as a move to go ahead with an internal settlement, were unanimously declared null and void by the Security Council.

Consultations between the United Nations and South Africa regarding the operational requirements for the deployment of the United Nations Transition Assistance Group began once again early in 1979. My special representative made a further visit to the territory and to Pretoria, as well as to the front-line states, i.e., those bordering on South Africa, to discuss outstanding problems. But as soon as one crucial problem was resolved, another arose to take its place. As I had suspected, the political will of the parties was insufficient to overcome their fears and preoccupations about the outcome of the UN operation. The uncertainty continued in spite of strenuous efforts by the five Western members of the Council, the front-line states and my staff and myself.

As I write this, it remains to be seen whether the United Nations plan for Namibia will be put into effect. I still hope that a peaceful solution satisfactory to all the parties can be found to save the country from further bloodshed. But a great deal of effort will have to be made first.

Negotiations to find a solution to the Rhodesian problem are equally complex. The parallels between Namibia and Zimbabwe (Southern Rhodesia) are obvious. The unilateral declaration of independence of the white minority in Rhodesia on 11 November 1965 was made in defiance of the African majority and the British government, which is the internationally recognized administering power, and was rejected by the United Nations. When its request that the British government use every means to restore its authority proved ineffective, the Security Council, on 16 December 1966, applied economic sanctions against the Smith régime, the first such action in UN history. While these sanctions have had the effect of weakening the régime, widespread evasion has prevented them from bringing about the desired result.

Thirteen years after its unilateral declaration of independence in the face of increasingly strong African and international pressure, the Salisbury régime finally conceded to the principle of majority rule. Proposals put forward by the American and British governments for the achievement of independence, however, have not been successful. Among other things, these proposals provide for the setting up of a transitional government, the peaceful transfer of governmental authority to the African majority, and guarantees for the white population.

Salisbury's negative attitude has led to a steady escalation of guerrilla activity and violent reprisals by the Rhodesian forces. Thousands of people have fled the territory and sought asylum in neighbouring countries. Because the liberation movements operate out of Mozambique and Zambia, these two countries have been the targets of attacks by Rhodesian planes and ground forces, with tragic consequences.

An additional complication has been the lack of agreement among the African leadership. Two principal groups led by

Nkomo and Mugabe have merged and become the Patriotic Front. This has gained them the support of the Organization of African Unity. The two remaining leaders, Bishop Muzorewa and the Reverend Sithole, decided, in March 1978, to opt for an internal settlement with Ian Smith, after the latter had publicly declared that he would accept a black majority government – a government, however, in which the white minority would maintain a controlling voice. The Security Council declared any such settlement illegal and unacceptable, and appealed to all states not to accord it recognition. Despite international condemnation, elections were held in April 1979 to carry the process of internal settlement a step further. The liberation movements, however, have increased their resistance.

In my view, a lasting solution to the problem can only come about if all political parties and liberation movements participate in the negotiating process for the achievement of independence. That was the aim of the Anglo-American proposals and, in March 1978, the Security Council requested me to nominate a personal representative to participate in further negotiations by the Western powers, with a view to the possible employment of UN peace-keeping troops. I appointed General Prem Chand, an excellent officer with long experience in UN peace-keeping operations, for the job. At the moment, however, it seems that the Western approach has been overtaken by events. All African leaders, with whom I have discussed the present situation in southern Africa, share the view that every effort towards a peaceful solution via negotiations must be undertaken if the peoples of the area are to be spared further hardship. The President of Zambia, Kenneth Kaunda, has long been trying to bring the antagonists to the negotiating table, as has President Julius Nyerere of Tanzania. Both leaders have assured me that neither wants bloodshed but they will not shirk their responsibility should the situation deteriorate further.

There can no longer be any doubt that self-determination and the establishment of majority rule, through fair and democratic processes, offer both Namibia and Zimbabwe the best guarantees for peace. Any denial of this process will only prolong the tragic situation in those territories which could well develop into a regional conflict. Our primary task must be to achieve a just and urgent solution to this grave problem on the basis of internationally accepted principles.

CHAPTER SEVEN

Cyprus

WHEN I DECIDED in February 1977 to fly to Cyprus the problems confronting that small republic were no less complex than when I had first visited it as secretary-general in 1972. Nevertheless, I had some grounds for optimism. There were signs of a thaw in the relations between the island's Greek and Turkish communities. The month before, for the first time in thirteen years, President Makarios and Rauf Denktash, leader of the Turkish community, had declared their willingness to meet, perhaps with an eye to the recently elected Carter administration's announced determination to use its influence to promote a solution of the Cyprus problem. Their first meeting, which had taken place on 27 January under the aegis of my special representative, the Peruvian diplomat Javier Perez de Cuellar, had gone well. In order to speed up the *rapprochement* and set new negotiations in motion, I proposed that their talks be continued in my presence.

My visit had been planned with the UN staff in Nicosia down to the last detail and was to form the conclusion to a previously arranged trip through the Middle East. I was scheduled to arrive in Cyprus on 12 February but, shortly before my departure for Nicosia, I was told the two ethnic groups could not agree on where my plane should land. The international airport in Nicosia, which was under UN control, had not been used since the 1974 hostilities and remained closed, despite the agreement reached under my auspices in August 1975 to reopen it for UN use, because the Turkish side felt unable, apparently for security reasons, to implement it. Each side insisted on receiving me at an airport in its own sector of the country. Neither would give in on a matter which both viewed as a fundamental question of symbolic importance. Archbishop Makarios wished to emphasize the authority of the Republic of Cyprus, of which he was the president, while Rauf Denktash wanted recognition of his rights as head of the autonomous state that had been proclaimed by him in the northern sector of the island after the 1974 intervention of Turkish forces.

I appealed to both parties. Why let a matter of protocol hinder them in achieving their common goal, namely, the restoration of harmony and collaboration between the peoples of Cyprus? They finally agreed that my plane could land at the Larnaca airport in the government-controlled zone, where representatives of President Makarios would receive me. Then I was to fly by helicopter to the Nicosia airport, where representatives of Mr Denktash awaited me. Later, when I left Cyprus, my plane took off from Nicosia international airport, where a runway had been fixed up for just that purpose. I mention all these details to show the kind of complications that occur at every turn in trying to find a settlement to the Cyprus problem. The mutual distrust that resulted from the bitter fighting of 1963 and 1964 continues; yet, the unity of the country, with reasonable local autonomy for both communities, must be achieved.

Since the Ottoman conquest of Cyprus in the sixteenth century, Greeks and Turks had co-existed there in relative peace until recently. The Porte (the Turkish rulers) had exercised a fairly tolerant system of government. In return for a certain levy, Cypriot Christians were allowed to practise their religion freely, the Greek Orthodox Church was permitted all spiritual and secular rights, and the archbishop was recognized as ethnarch, i.e., elected leader and spokesman of the Greek Cypriot population. In 1878, the island came under British administration, although it remained a Turkish possession until the outbreak of war in 1914, when Britain annexed it. In 1924, Cyprus was formally made a British crown colony.

Over the centuries, sporadic attempts at independence on the part of the Greeks had been forcibly suppressed, but such incidents had never caused lasting damage to relations between the two Cypriot communities. Deterioration of that relationship began in the early 1930s and accelerated in the 1950s, when the *enosis* movement for unification with Greece gained increasing support among Greek Cypriots. Inasmuch as the island was then still a colony, EOKA, the Greek underground group advocating *enosis*, directed its activities against the British. But the concept of *enosis* alienated the Turkish Cypriots, who favoured decolonization but not annexation by Greece. Instead, they demanded *taksim* (partition of Cyprus between Greece and Turkey).

To find a way out of the impasse, the British government, in June 1955, invited Greece and Turkey to discuss the future of the island. Internationalizing the problem, however, led to new complications. The Turkish government, under Prime Minister Menderes, based its claim to co-determination in Cyprus on arguments that are still presented today, namely, the security of Turkey, whose coastline is scarcely sixty kilometres from Cyprus, and the protection of the Turkish Cypriot community. For Menderes, there were only two possibilities: maintenance of British rule or partition of the island between Turkey and Greece.

Neither of those solutions proved practicable, but after long negotiations some compromises acceptable to all were finally worked out by Menderes and Greek Prime Minister Karamanlis. These were the Zurich and London treaties of establishment, alliance, and guarantee of 1959 and 1960 under which Cyprus was established as an independent state whose integrity and security were guaranteed by all three powers. Britain would retain two sovereign base areas in Cyprus, while Greece and Turkey would each enjoy special relations with the new republic, including the stationing of army units on the island to train the Cypriot army.

A complicated constitution containing 199 articles went into force, guaranteeing the Turkish Cypriot community certain entrenched rights, special representation in the executive branch of the government, double majorities in the legislature, and the power of veto in specific matters of national interest, such as taxation and foreign affairs. Makarios was elected president, and Greek Cypriots (who comprised 81 per cent of the population) enjoyed a substantial majority in both the cabinet and the legislature. As might be expected, the representational ratios favouring the Greek Cypriots clashed with the special rights of the Turkish Cypriots, bringing about violent conflicts. In three years' time, the country was in a state of turmoil. In 1964, the United Nations sent a peace-keeping force (UNFICYP) to restore peace and maintain order, while it pursued its diplomatic efforts to help the parties reconcile their differences.

It was in 1972 that I first saw our peace-keeping troops in Cyprus at work. Their admirable impartiality and the intelligence and selflessness with which they exercised their duties were visible proof of the usefulness of the United Nations. The devoted activity of these men, popularly called the Blue Berets, is carried out without fanfare; yet daily they risk their lives to prevent conflicts and avert crises that could easily affect the peace and security of the entire globe.

At the time of my first visit, despite negotiations carried out under UN auspices for four years, there had been no accommodation on either side; whenever agreement seemed imminent, some last-minute hitch caused one or the other parties to withdraw, and work had to start again from scratch. Certainly, the positions of both sides were widely separated. For the Greek Cypriot community, it was a matter of preserving the unitary character of the state and securing the functions of government through application of the majority principle. The Turkish Cypriot community, on the other hand, insisted that the institutions of government be established in such a way that its prerogatives, its local autonomy and its security be guaranteed. Turkish leaders repeatedly maintained that Cyprus, unlike most other states, was composed of two ethnic groups that should enjoy equal status. While some Cypriots feared that negotiations would bring about partition of the island, whereby part would fall to Turkey, others suspected that Makarios was pursuing a secret strategy for eventual annexation of the entire country by Greece.

After talks with government officials in Nicosia, Ankara and Athens that summer of 1972, I realized that the prospects for negotiations were not favourable. Although Cyprus appeared outwardly calm, fresh conflicts seemed likely. That is why I disagreed when some UN member states suggested the peace-keeping force be withdrawn or at least limited for reasons of economy. Relations between Makarios and the military régime in Athens were strained. I was quite aware of that, because several months earlier I had helped to settle a serious crisis between the two governments, when Athens had not only called upon the Cypriot president to reform his cabinet in order to include some well-known supporters of *enosis* but had also demanded the disarmament of the Cypriot police force and the strengthening of the National Guard, which was under the command of Greek officers and was secretly being armed with imported weapons.

Turkey immediately accused Makarios of violating the 1960 agreement, which provided for a certain balance between the two communities, and threatened to supply the Turkish Cypriots with weapons in turn. Suddenly the United Nations was in a very delicate position. We could not be a party to the Greek junta's desire to keep Makarios disarmed, but we were equally concerned about Makarios' import of weapons which could easily be used against the Turkish Cypriot community. After lengthy negotiations in March 1972, we persuaded Makarios to store the imported weapons in depots to which the Greek Cypriots would have access only with the consent of UN representatives. Jointly carried out inspections further contributed to calming the two sides; but it was obvious that the tensions would re-emerge.

In the autumn of 1972, a plot was discovered to oust the Makarios government. The conspirators belonged to EOKA-B, a pro-*enosis* faction supported by the National Guard and headed by General Grivas, leader of the earlier struggle against the British. In the months that followed there were frequent clashes between the government and EOKA-B forces. We received reports of heavy fighting in the mountain regions, of local police stations being stormed and destroyed and arms depots plundered. Time bombs exploded in various localities. Finally, the Cypriot minister of justice was kidnapped. In spite of the government's retaliation and mop-up operations, including the dismissal of a number of National Guard officers, rumours were rife that a *coup d'état* was imminent.

Faced with the opposition of EOKA-B and its strong bid for popular support, Makarios found himself obliged to harden his position in the intercommunal talks which had earlier offered such a good chance for success. On 15 July 1974, the *coup d'état*, organized by the military régime in Athens, did, in fact, take place. Curiously enough, it provoked no immediate action by the Security Council or the Cypriot delegate to the United Nations. I was carrying out consultations to enable the convening of the Council when we learned that the Archbishop, whose death had been announced by the conspirators, had escaped the bombing of his palace and had managed to flee Nicosia. I immediately instructed our peace-keeping troops to guarantee his safety. Shortly afterwards, he left Cyprus on a British plane. Later, in New York, he told me that he had read with some amusement the various obituaries that had been prematurely printed.

Turkey, as was to be expected, was profoundly disturbed by the change of government in Nicosia, which it considered a prelude to annexation by Greece. The self-proclaimed Greek Cypriot president, Nikos Sampson, was a member of EOKA-B and a known supporter of *enosis*. The Turkish press gave great play to his role in the fierce guerrilla attacks against the Turkish Cypriots in 1963 and 1964. Even as the situation was being debated in the Security Council, which had been convened on my initiative, it became evident that Turkey had no intention of awaiting further developments. Under the terms of the 1960 treaty, Turkey, Greece, and the United Kingdom had the right to intervene in Cyprus and restore constitutional order. Its two bases gave Britain the technical means and necessary logistic equipment for such an operation. Moreover, units of the Royal Navy were then cruising off the Cypriot coast. For a number of reasons, however, the British government declined Turkish Prime Minister Ecevit's proposal that the two governments undertake a joint military intervention on the basis of the 1960 treaty.

On 20 July 1974, only five days after the overthrow of President Makarios, Turkish troops landed in Cyprus. The Security Council held an urgent meeting that same day, demanding an end of fighting, withdrawal of the invading force, restoration of the constitutional government, and respect for the independence and territorial integrity of Cyprus. The Turkish expeditionary force, however, continued its advance from Kyrenia and reached the outskirts of Nicosia. The capital's airport was badly damaged and put out of operation. On 23 July, I sent both sides an urgent appeal for the immediate cessation of hostilities. That same day, the Security Council repeated its call for a cease-fire. But the fighting went on, despite the collapse of the military régime in Athens on 23 July and Sampson's resignation in Nicosia. Constitutional legality was restored in Nicosia by designating the speaker of the Cypriot legislature, Glafkos Clerides, as acting head of state pending the return of President Makarios the following December.

I have been often asked, 'Why didn't the UN peace-keeping troops intervene at the time to restore peace?' This ignores the fact that they had been sent to Cyprus solely to maintain peace between the two ethnic communities. Our mandate in no way authorized intervention – nor did our Force have the capability to oppose heavily armed foreign troops or to enter into conflict with them. If that had been so, many member states would certainly have refused to provide contingents. The UN Force was instructed to protect the civilian population as much as possible from the effects of the fighting, which put a great strain on our relations with the Turkish army, and even here a real confrontation arose over the question of control of the international airport in Nicosia. The UN representative and the Force commander requested both sides to refrain from attacking the airport in order to avoid additional civilian casualties and great material loss. After lengthy negotiations under the UN flag, the leader of the Cypriot National Guard and the local commander of the Turkish forces reached an agreement whereby the Cypriot National Guard relinquished its positions on the airport grounds to the UN troops, the Turkish army promised no further attacks, and an armistice went into effect immediately in the airport sector occupied by UN contingents.

My relief over this arrangement was, unfortunately, short-lived. Only twenty-four hours later I learned that the local Turkish commander had ordered our troops to leave the airport. If they didn't, his men would attack. Clearly that put the United Nations in an intolerable position. It was impossible for me to go back on the assurance I had given the Greek Cypriots and violate an agreement made in good faith. Had I done so, the United Nations would have lost all credibility. I was thus forced to conclude that, under the circumstances, the Blue Berets would have to defend the airport.

In that extraordinarily tense situation, my personal relations with the Turkish prime minister stood me in good stead. I persuaded Bulent Ecevit to order his army to respect the local armistice agreed on. Nicosia airport remained under UN control and, in that sector, at least, further bloodshed was avoided.

By the end of July, inasmuch as the Security Council had not succeeded in ending the conflict, the foreign ministers of Great

Britain, Greece, and Turkey, the three signatory states of the 1960 treaty, began intensive negotiations in Geneva. They agreed on the setting up of a security zone under UNFICYP control at the limit of the areas occupied by the Turkish armed forces and on the evacuation of Turkish enclaves occupied by Greek or Greek Cypriot forces. UNFICYP was to provide protection to these enclaves and also to villages of mixed ethnic groups. Having obtained the endorsement of the Security Council of that role for UNFICYP, I instructed my special representative and the Force commander to proceed carrying out its plans. Some progress was made, and on 12 August the National Guard began evacuating Turkish Cypriot villages. The Geneva Conference, however, broke down because of the non-negotiable demand by the Turkish side for territory that far exceeded the area already controlled by Turkish forces. On the morning of 14 August 1974, the Turkish army resumed its advance. Only after it had occupied the entire northern section of the island, approximately 36 per cent of the country, was Ankara prepared to obey the renewed cease-fire order of the Security Council.

At the end of August, I went to Cyprus, Greece and Turkey to explore the possibilities for a political solution. In Cyprus, my first task was to mitigate the worst effects of the war; some 200,000 Greek Cypriots – more than one third of the population – had fled the battle areas in the north and sought refuge in the south. They had lost all their possessions and were living in great need. An attempt had to be made to restore contact between the two communities. By emphasizing the purely humanitarian problems, I was able to arrange a meeting between Clerides and Denktash. Denktash went with me in a UN vehicle across the demarcation line into the Greek sector of Nicosia for the meeting with Clerides, which proved extremely useful. The two men began a dialogue that was to continue over the coming months.

In my subsequent talks with him in Ankara, I came to recognize Prime Minister Ecevit as a realistic and, in some ways, conciliatory statesman. I felt that he was ready to make concessions that might have opened the way for a compromise solution. A short time after, however, Ecevit resigned, and so no practical results came of those consultations.

Several nations, among them the United States, tried vainly to bring about a solution. The Soviet proposal that an international conference on the future of Cyprus be convened was rejected by Turkey, which insisted that the internal problems of Cyprus be solved by the Cypriots themselves.

Against that background, the Security Council, in a resolution adopted on 12 March 1975, recommended that negotiations between the two communities be resumed and entrusted me with a new mission to that end. I was to convene the parties under newly agreed procedures and place myself at their disposal.

The mission, which I began in early 1975, proved difficult from the outset. The conference site alone created problems. President Makarios suggested New York, but Denktash disagreed. He argued that since the Greek Cypriots were the accredited representatives of Cyprus to the United Nations, the Turkish Cypriots would have no comparable representation. For similar reasons, he excluded Rome, Paris, and Geneva. After a month of intensive discussions both delegations finally settled on Vienna, where the Republic of Cyprus had no diplomatic representation. Clerides and Denktash continued as interlocutors for their respective sides.

Between 1975 and 1977, there were six rounds of negotiations under my chairmanship, without a satisfactory solution being found. Even at the first round of talks, which began on 28 April 1975, the extent of the differences became obvious. The Greek Cypriots demanded that the Turkish troops withdraw, that the unitary character of the Republic and a strong central government be maintained, and that extensive territorial concessions be made by the Turkish Cypriots, who, with the support of Turkish troops, were still occupying more than 36 per cent of the country. The Turkish Cypriots insisted that the problem of a constitution had to be solved first. The autonomy they were demanding must be precisely defined; also, the structure of the two future federated states must be clearly formulated, since each was to have such far-reaching self-administration. Unlike the Greek Cypriots, the Turks favoured a fairly weak central government, with strictly limited powers. To get the dialogue under way, I invited both sides, first, to state their views concerning the territorial limits of the two federated states. But neither side wanted to commit itself publicly. Six days later, the meeting ended without agreement having been reached on any of the issues raised.

During the second negotiating phase in June of the same year, I tried a different tack. I brought up a problem which, although marginal, was nevertheless symbolically important: the reopening of the international airport at Nicosia. Here, at least, an initial success could be scored, I hoped, for both sides were basically in favour of resuming international air traffic. What they could not agree on was who was to administer the airport. My suggestion was to transfer the airport's operation for the time being to the United Nations. This proved unacceptable to either side.

During the third meeting, which began in late July and carried over into August 1975, both delegations were prepared to discuss the refugee question. To my great satisfaction, a first agreement was reached: all Turkish Cypriots residing in the Greek Cypriot sector received the right to settle in the north, which was under control of the Turkish army; the resettlement task was entrusted to UNFICYP. In return, Rauf Denktash was prepared to give the Greek Cypriots living in the Turkish sector certain safeguards, including freedom of movement, free exercise of religion, independent schooling, medical care and free access to UN representatives.

Consequently, more than 8,000 Turks did, in fact, migrate to the northern part of the island. The Greeks, on the other hand, received scarcely any of the anticipated facilities and in great numbers gave up their homes in the Turkish-occupied sector to migrate, often under destitute conditions, to the south. By 1977, out of the 10,000 Greeks who had initially elected to remain in the Turkish zone despite the fighting, only 1,800 were left.

The fourth meeting, held in New York in September 1975, yielded little progress.

The Greek Cypriot exodus from the north further taxed relations between the two ethnic groups. But I refused to be disheartened, and during the fifth phase of negotiations in February 1976 again urged both delegations to put forward their concrete ideas for a solution to the territorial question. To everyone's surprise, Glafkos Clerides pulled a map out of his file and showed us the settlement areas occupied by the Turkish army which the Greeks wanted back to accommodate their refugees. He made it clear that his suggestion should in no way be interpreted as a territorial proposal. At our request, he gave Denktash and me copies of the map that same evening. The next day it was agreed that the two parties would exchange detailed proposals in writing within six weeks. Now it seemed that we were finally on the road to genuine dialogue! But Clerides' resignation as spokesman for the Greek Cypriots in April 1976, the result of tensions within the government and a leakage of the arrangements he had agreed to in Nicosia, put an abrupt end to the Vienna negotiations. Once more we had to start afresh.

In September 1976, I invited the new representatives of the two communities, Tassos Papadopoulos and Umit Suleiman Onan, to New York. But the very first exchange of views strengthened my conviction that the conditions for a resumption of the dialogue were not at hand.

Only in December 1976 was there again a glimmer of hope, when my representative in Nicosia passed on the news that Denktash wished for a meeting with Makarios and that Perez de Cuellar was to arrange the talks. This new developement was all the more astounding in that both sides had previously shrunk from such a meeting. Makarios had, in effect, renounced *enosis* but still insisted on the unitary character of the state and considered the formation of a strong central government as the prerequisite of a federation. Until that moment, it had seemed inconceivable that he would consent to negotiate with the representative of the 'minority' as an equal partner. The Turkish Cypriots, for their part, were opposed to negotiating with a man who was both president and archbishop, since they believed in the total separation of church and state. Consequently, since the events of 1963–64, there had been almost no contact between Makarios and the Turkish Cypriot leaders.

Perez de Cuellar delivered to Makarios the Denktash request for a personal meeting. Taken by surprise, the Archbishop asked for time to think it over. In the end, Makarios and Denktash finally met twice on the neutral territory of the United Nations in Nicosia. At the first meeting, on 27 January 1977, my special representative was present; the second meeting, on 12 February, took place under my auspices. The talks were not only friendly but also encouraging. For the first time, the leader of the Turkish group voluntarily brought the territorial question under discussion, which, in the eyes of the Greek Cypriots, was a matter of cardinal importance to any further settlement. Denktash went so far as to offer, within the framework of a comprehensive settlement, the restoration of part of the sector under his control. He concretely proposed reducing the sector occupied by the Turks from more than 36 per cent of the island to 32.8 per cent. The Archbishop considered this concession inadequate. In his opinion, the partition of the territory should correspond to the population ratio, which meant the Greeks should own 80 per cent of Cyprus and the Turks 20 per cent. Still, he did not rule out further negotiations.

These discussions took place in a considerably more friendly atmosphere than had former meetings between the two groups. There was even talk of outlining a future federation under a central government. The latter would be responsible for foreign policy, national defence and financial matters. The two leaders also agreed on written guidelines for the course of further negotiations. At last nothing appeared to stand in the way of resuming the Vienna talks.

On the basis of the Makarios-Denktash guidelines, Cyprus would become an independent, non-aligned federal republic, consisting of two ethnic groups. The size of the territory administered by each group was to be negotiated according to economic viability and productivity and the existing ownership of land. Fundamental questions, such as freedom of movement and freedom to settle and own property, were to be the subject of discussion that would take into account the principle of a bicommunal federal system and certain practical difficulties that might arise for the Turkish Cypriot group. The task of the central government was to safeguard both the unity of the country and the bicommunal character of the state.

Both parties had quite obviously recognized the need for a solution based on mutual concessions. They also seemed to understand that their future as a country depended on a co-existence profitable for both sides. My personal interventions and those of my representatives, as well as the proposals of various friendly powers, had probably contributed to that welcome development.

On leaving Nicosia in February 1977, I felt as if the United Nations had accomplished a great deal; all the same I realized that it would be some time before a settlement could be reached. That became even clearer during the sixth round of talks that April in Vienna, which brought no progress.

The sudden death of President Makarios, whose strong personality had put its stamp upon events for nearly forty years, created a new situation. The unanimous election of his former foreign minister, Spiros Kyprianou, brought to the head of the Republic an active man whom I had known well for many years. In Turkey, too, at almost the same time, there was a change of government, and Bulent Ecevit resumed the office of prime minister.

In order to get the negotiations moving again, in January 1978 I visited all the countries concerned. In Ankara, Ecevit assured me that he would shortly present concrete proposals for the solution of the Cyprus problem. He refused to go into any details on the grounds that such proposals could only be worked out after his approval as prime minister by the Turkish legislature. During my subsequent visit to Nicosia, it was agreed among Kyprianou, Denktash and myself that the Turkish Cypriot proposals should first be submitted to me, as secretary-general of the United Nations. That way I could study them and, after consulting with both sides, decide when next to convene a round of talks between the two communities.

Suddenly there were all sorts of difficulties. The Turkish proposals, which were to have been available at the end of February, were not ready until the middle of April. The Turkish document handed to me on 13 April in Vienna contained concrete proposals, especially concerning the future constitution of Cyprus, and a series of indications of the geographic regions where the Turkish Cypriot leadership was prepared to negotiate territorial concessions. The latter included part of the Greek Cypriot sector of Famagusta; the Turkish proposals provided for the return of the Greek population to that sector, but under Turkish administration. Ecevit and Denktash informed me that those were their starting positions and could be negotiated further during the discussions.

I assumed that it would take about an hour for the Turkish Cypriot documents to be submitted to me in Vienna. The Turkish Cypriot representative, Mumtaz Soysal, had other ideas. He suggested that I make a public declaration, in which I would describe the proposals as a useful basis for negotiations. I was then to announce the imminent resumption of negotiations. It was quite clear the Turkish Cypriot side thought consulting with the Greek Cypriots concerning the content of the proposals was not necessary and that only the technical aspects of the next round of talks need be discussed with them. I, on the contrary, had made it clear ever since my visit to Nicosia in January that the agreement between Kyprianou and Denktash called for prior consultation with both sides and only their agreement could bring about resumption of the talks. I also pointed out that it would not be very practical to organize negotiations if one side were to reject the basis for them as unsatisfactory. In view of this, it was not surprising that it finally took three meetings, lasting seven hours, to agree on one short communiqué, which simply stated that the Turkish Cypriot proposals dealt with the constitutional and territorial aspects of the Cyprus problem in a concrete way – which was not a judgement as to their merits. I told Soysal that I would study the proposals carefully and would be in touch with both sides.

In assessing the Cyprus situation at that moment, one aspect extraneous to the negotiating process must also be taken into account, namely, the American arms embargo imposed against Turkey in 1975. Ankara was keen to have it lifted as soon as possible. In the light of the Carter administration's proposal in early 1978 for lifting of the embargo, resumption of the negotiating process took on enormous importance for the Turkish side. The Greek Cypriots, however, were little inclined to agree to negotiations from which they expected nothing or very little.

Given the situation, I decided it best to deliver the Turkish Cypriot proposals to Kyprianou personally on my way back from a forthcoming Middle East journey. That way I could discuss with him the question of resuming the intercommunal talks. It seemed to me an important and practical move, as I had planned to go on from Vienna to visit our UN troops in southern Lebanon and to have talks in Beirut and Israel. My time was short, as I had to return to New York as quickly as possible to report to the Security Council on the situation in southern Lebanon; but I did manage to stop over in Cyprus on 19 April to make the planned delivery and, subsequently, have a discussion with Denktash.

Kyprianou and I met for two hours. He informed me that the Turkish proposals were wholly unacceptable as a basis for new negotiations. He also voiced his fear that the territorial concessions offered by the Turks would be taken as an insult by the Greek population and that the Turkish suggestions concerning a constitution would, in fact, lead to a complete division of the island. It was clear that his government was not prepared to take part in a new round of talks. I could not dissuade Kyprianou from that negative attitude, but urged him to do nothing that might irrevocably wreck the resumption of talks. I returned to New York convinced once more that we were at an impasse.

Under the circumstances, it was important for me to maintain my credibility as impartial mediator. Since the positions of both sides were diamentrically opposed, I could do nothing except stress the usefulness of direct negotiations and indicate that the convening of intercommunal talks could be meaningful only if both sides agreed to make them so. I made it clear that I could not force the issue, and repeated my willingness to maintain contact between all parties involved and to continue every effort to set the negotiating process in motion again. To that end I used the special session of the General Assembly on disarmament questions in early 1978, in which President Kyprianou and Prime Ministers Ecevit and Karamanlis took part, to assess the latest state of affairs. Rauf Denktash was also in New York, but, unfortunately, I could not get them all around the table. Kyprianou was only interested in meeting Ecevit, who declined the overture because he did not recognize Kyprianou as the head of state of Cyprus. Denktash, for his part, was interested in talks with Kyprianou, who, however, declined such a meeting because he feared that it would be interpreted as a *de facto* recognition of Denktash as president of the so-called Turkish Federated State of Cyprus. And so the opportunity to close the gap by means of personal discussion was lost.

In reporting on the impasse to the Security Council at the end of May 1978, I mentioned the difficulty of evolving a genuine negotiating process out of the parties' conflicting positions and suggested a new approach. Why not try to eliminate certain anomalous situations that had posed obstacles in the way of earlier attempts to deal with the broader problem? I specifically had in mind Varosha, the Greek Cypriot sector of Famagusta, which remained in an empty and decaying state under Turkish occupation. With the assistance of UNFICYP, could not the town be reopened, resettled, and rehabilitated?

My suggestion led to intensive consultations with all the parties and to an offer by Denktash allowing Varosha to be resettled by its Greek Cypriot inhabitants under an interim UN administration – but only upon resumption of negotiations. Additional ideas were proffered by the United States, which indicated a great interest in achieving progress on the Cyprus question.

Beginning in December 1978, I worked out a series of suggestions in an effort to provide some mutually acceptable basis for resumption of the intercommunal talks. The positions of the parties remained intractable, however, with the Turkish Cypriots insisting on unilateral action by the Greek Cypriots to lift the 'economic blockade' on the Turkish Cypriot area, and the Greek Cypriots demanding the resettlement of Varosha first. Finally, not without misgivings over the chances of success, I asked the leaders of the two communities – Kyprianou and Denktash – to meet with me in Nicosia on my return from a visit to the Far East to try to cut the Gordian knot concerning resumption of the talks.

This high-level meeting took place on 18 and 19 May 1979. Negotiations proved intensive and, at times, very difficult. I tried to press upon both sides the feeling of the international community that it was time, at long last, to move towards a settlement – or at least towards some initial practical measures. Surprisingly enough, these efforts were successful; a ten-point agreement was arrived at under which the talks would be resumed on 15 June, priority being given to the resettlement of Varosha and to the adoption of initial practical measures by both sides to promote good will, mutual confidence and a return to normal conditions.

The Cyprus problem, unique in so many ways, is one of the most complicated and emotionally loaded of our time. In assessing its importance, however, the geopolitical situation of the island must be taken into account, as only in that way do the international ramifications become understandable. Naturally, I shall continue my efforts, but I have no doubt that the road to a solution will be long and difficult. Ultimately, as always, success depends on the good will of the parties themselves.

CHAPTER EIGHT

The Middle East

It was from our military observers in the Middle East that we learned in the early morning of 6 October 1973 that full-scale fighting had broken out again. Soon after, I received a telephone call from Henry Kissinger, urging me to use my influence in that part of the world to prevent the fighting from spreading.

My quick telephone calls to the representatives of the countries involved and the reports which came in from the United Nations observation posts confirmed that the fourth Arab-Israeli war was well under way.

It was clear that neither the American nor the Israeli intelligence services had expected the Egyptian-Syrian offensive. The military preparations that had been going on for several months had remained unknown to them, or at least had not been taken seriously.

Looking back, it seems strange that no one had heeded the Egyptian and Syrian warnings that they intended to regain the territories occupied by Israel in 1967. The Egyptian government had made a final attempt in July 1973 to resolve the issue through United Nations channels. It had demanded a meeting of the Security Council to examine the Middle East problem from a global viewpoint and to find the way towards a peaceful settlement. During the heated debates, Egyptian Foreign Minister Mohamed Hassan El Zayyat had stated that his country would be forced to resort to other means if the Council proved incapable of solving the problem in accordance with the long-standing decisions of the United Nations concerning the occupied territories. In talks with me, El Zayyat had also hinted at such action, but the import of his statements seems to have eluded us all.

Inasmuch as the meeting of the Security Council had yielded nothing constructive, I decided to visit the area the following September, hoping that personal contact with the leaders of the states involved might in some way help the situation. It was during that trip that I came to realize at first hand how vast was the abyss separating the two sides.

Golda Meir, then prime minister of Israel, was the dominant figure in Israeli politics, passionately devoted to her people and direct in her approach to problems. Her conviction of the correctness of her policies was matched only by her profound distrust of the Arabs. She rejected any compromise that in her eyes could damage Israel. She was the personification of Israel's determination to survive and command respect.

At our first meeting, she reproached me for having stated in the introduction to my recently published Annual Report to the General Assembly that the Middle East situation was 'explosive' and that the danger of war would not subside so long as the stalemate in negotiations continued. She expressed her displeasure quite frankly, saying that if only the United Nations would refrain from interfering in the affairs of the Middle East, in two or three years the Arabs would be prepared to recognize the State of Israel and to concede it the borders which it believed essential to its security. I made it quite clear that I did not share her views and drew her attention to the information available to us from our observers and from other sources which indicated that the situation was rapidly worsening. I cited the growing unrest in the Arab countries, their impatience to regain the areas lost in 1967 and the size and disposition of their military forces. Although at that time I could not guess that in only a month a new war would break out, I left Mrs Meir with the conviction that the Israeli leadership was making a grave mistake in ignoring the feeling of its adversaries. I also felt that Israel seriously underestimated the military potential and fighting spirit of its enemies. Their victory in 1967 had led many Israelis to assume that they could easily deal with any Arab military initiative. Unfortunately, it required a new round of fighting to induce the Israeli leadership to modify its views somewhat.

Of all the Israeli politicians I met at that time, Abba Eban was the one I knew best. During his long period as Israeli ambassador in Washington and permanent representative at the United Nations, I had frequently heard him speak. One did not have to agree with him to acknowledge his intellect, his oratorical skill, and his urbane manner. In his basic attitudes, Eban was perhaps no less firm than Mrs Meir, but he expressed his views more diplomatically.

My relations with Eban's successor, Yigal Allon, were in some ways simpler. He always made a distinction between the United Nations Middle East resolutions, many of which, like his predecessors, he rejected, and the activities of the Secretariat and of the UN peace-keeping forces along the cease-fire lines. In particular, I appreciated the public recognition he repeatedly gave to the Blue Berets for their difficult and thankless task. I always had the impression that Allon understood the difficulty of my position both as spokesman for the United Nations in an emotionally-charged conflict and as the executive responsible for the Organization's practical, day-to-day operations.

During that same trip in September 1973, I also visited Beirut, Damascus, Amman, and Cairo. Both President Sadat and President Assad welcomed me warmly, but I was somewhat puzzled by their disinclination to talk. Only later did I realize that they had already decided to mount a military operation, and thus it was difficult for them to discuss the negotiating process in detail without revealing their intentions. On my next visit to Egypt in June 1974, Sadat explained his earlier reticence. He had, he said, given the Security Council adequate warning of the seriousness of the situation in the previous July, and no one could have expected him to have said more concerning his intentions. Moreover, all of Egypt's military preparations had been carried out in full view of the world, particularly Israel, which had been conducting daily reconnaissance fights along the Suez Canal zone. He thought it significant that world opinion had been so sceptical of Arab military capacity and determination.

In many ways, the October war of 1973 represented a turning point, not only in the history of the Arab-Israeli conflict but in the history of the United Nations. From the moment the fighting began, and as it continued, the United Nations repeatedly urged all parties to cease their military activities. Only on 22 October, however, when the conflict showed dangerous signs of escalating, did the Security Council adopt Resolution 338, calling for an immediate cease-fire and the immediate start of peace negotiations between the two sides. But the fighting did not stop, and it became clear that peace could only be restored by sending UN troops in to supervise a cease-fire. It was another three days before a resolution elaborated by eight of the non-aligned members of the Council was adopted, authorizing the dispatch of UN troops.

The imminent threat of a Soviet-American confrontation had, meanwhile, alarmed the world. The demand made by the Soviet Union on 23 October that Israel comply with Resolution 338 and rumours of Soviet troop movements prompted President Nixon to place US troops on the alert the following day. Press reports that the CIA had information indicating that the Soviet Union was preparing to intervene in Egypt contributed to creating an extremely tense situation, and it was in this atmosphere that both Moscow and Washington agreed to the dispatch of a UN emergency force to the Middle East.

Immediately that decision had been made and I was authorized by the Council to act, I moved to organize the operation. Seldom before had the United Nations acted so swiftly and so successfully. Overnight, the necessary guidelines were drawn up for authorization by the Council the next morning. For the first time, East European soldiers – Poles – were to be included in the UN force, which would be financed out of regular assessments of the United Nations membership. It was also decided that only the Security Council would have the right to withdraw the troops at such time as might appear justified.

In view of the relative quiet prevailing in Cyprus, I decided to transfer a large number of the UN troops stationed there to the front lines in the Middle East. With the aid of the British air force, the first UN contingents were interposed between the Egyptian and Israeli forces within twenty-four hours of the Council's decision. As the cease-fire decision was now largely observed, the necessary preconditions for opening negotiations were created. Those talks began two months later in Geneva.

The United Nations played an important role in the process of establishing negotiating relations between Israel and Egypt. It was the United Nations that made it possible for the military authorities of both countries to meet at kilometre 101 on the Cairo-Suez road, first to arrange for the exchange of prisoners and supply convoys to the beleaguered Egyptian army and, later, after the Geneva Conference, to conclude the final agreement on the separation of forces. On the basis of those negotiations, which could only take place in the presence of UN representatives, an agreement was reached on 18 January 1974 whereby the Israeli troops withdrew thirty kilometres from the east bank of the Suez Canal. The Egyptian troops positioned on the east bank were correspondingly limited. At the same time, a buffer zone was set up between the two armies which has been occupied since that time by UN troops.

Our actions during and after the October war impressed Henry Kissinger. Previously, he had not been an enthusiastic supporter of the United Nations and had often declared his preference for bilateral diplomacy rather than multilateral negotiations in settling international conflicts. As a pronounced individualist, aware of his position and his own capabilities, he liked to solve problems on his own, backed, of course, by the power and influence of his government. But the October war proved conclusively that the United Nations could perform valuable services. Kissinger came to realize that there were certain tasks, such as peace-keeping, which could not be executed unilaterally, even by a great power, and that, in such cases, the United Nations could be of great service.

I have always regarded bilateral and multilateral diplomacy as complementary elements in world politics. Developments after the October war supported that view, for it very soon became obvious that the Geneva Conference was not leading to a peace treaty. Syria declined to participate, and neither the other Arab states nor Israel were ready for genuine dialogue. It was then that Henry Kissinger made a great contribution on a bilateral level by proposing that Israel and its neighbours, Egypt and Syria, conclude interim agreements. In so doing, he held a trump card: both sides trusted and needed the United States and its secretary of state. The Israelis preferred Kissinger's negotiations to the Geneva Conference, and the Arabs recognized that the United States was the only power with enough influence to persuade Israel to make concessions on the question of disengagement. The shuttle diplomacy of the American secretary of state was later to prove an important element within the framework of Resolutions 242 and 338 as a step towards the solution to the Middle East conflict.

Kissinger kept me up to date on his efforts and their results. His numerous journeys, his endless discussions with the leaders of the Middle East countries involved many setbacks before they finally led to the separation of forces agreements in the Sinai Peninsula and on the Golan Heights. He never lost his *sang-froid* or his sense of humour, even during the most strenuous moments of negotiation.

Before he resigned as secretary of state in January 1977 prior to the inauguration of the Carter administration, Kissinger paid me a farewell visit at the United Nations. Congratulating me on my election to a second term of office as secretary-general, he jokingly commented, 'Your re-election, Kurt, proves that you are better at managing elections than we are!'

By that time, it seemed that the policy of shuttle diplomacy had had its day, and that it might be worthwhile to consider resumption of the Geneva Conference. The Middle East journey I undertook in February 1977 to study the reactions of the governments to that proposal confirmed my beliefs. All the Arab leaders with whom I met were in favour of a new peace conference in Geneva and urged that it be convened as soon as possible. President Sadat, for example, assured me that he attached no value to formalities or protocol that might delay the convening of the conference. His only concern was to get to a solution of the problem as quickly as possible. In this connection he was much concerned with the question of Israel's true intentions and feared that the Rabin government might be tempted to maintain the *status quo* by delaying negotiations, in order to continue the establishment of settlements in the occupied areas. Though a great supporter of Kissinger's shuttle diplomacy, Sadat constantly emphasized the importance of including the United Nations in the negotiations. But if the Geneva Conference could not be reconvened, then Egypt – as Foreign Minister Ismail Fahmy stressed – would turn again to the Security Council, as it had done in July 1973.

In all the talks I have had with Sadat over the years I have been impressed by his honesty and frankness. He is not one to shrink from admitting past errors and pointing out the blunders and missed opportunities that have characterized the Middle East conflict. He has explained to me, time and again, that he wants to create peace in the Middle East once and for all. It required great courage on his part to conclude the second withdrawal agreement with Israel on the Sinai Peninsula in September 1975. In the face of growing criticism, he steadfastly defended his view that the Arab world must act realistically to achieve a peaceful solution.

Sadat recognized that Israel would give up the occupied areas only if it obtained peace and security. He made no attempt to disguise the fact that a peaceful solution would benefit Egypt, which would never overcome its economic and social problems until it could stop allocating so much of its budget to military expenses. Sadat tried to convince the Arab world that the path of compromise he had elected to pursue would lead eventually to peace. He followed that line of reasoning with his dramatic visit to Jerusalem in November 1977 and in the subsequent negotiations leading to the conclusion of the Egypt-Israel peace treaty.

Syrian President Hafez al Assad is much more reserved by nature than Sadat and approaches every problem with extreme caution. Over the years a trusting relationship has developed between us. Though somewhat patriarchal in manner, he is always kind and listens patiently and sympathetically to others, even when he does not share their views. Although basically desiring peace, he is firm when the interests of his country are at stake.

Like other Arab leaders, President Assad's ground-rule conditions for peace are, first, the restitution of all the territories Israel has occupied since 1967 and, second, recognition of the Palestinians' right to self-determination in their own state. From my talks with him in February 1977, I realized that he viewed Israel's willingness to negotiate seriously far more sceptically than did Sadat. King Hussein also expressed deep concern over Israel's policies in the occupied areas. To him the steadily growing number of Israeli settlements on the west bank of the Jordan was a most unfavourable sign. How could one trust the Israeli leaders, he asked me, so long as they continued to create one *fait accompli* after another, to place one obstacle after another in the path of a peaceful solution? The Jordanian ruler made it clear to me that the Arab world was becoming more and more impatient, the people more demanding of explanations from their leaders. He wanted the Geneva Conference convened and a peace agreement reached as soon as possible; otherwise, in his opinion, the situation could only worsen.

In Lebanon, President Sarkis discussed with me the special problems facing his country: an end to Lebanon's bitter civil war and the restoration of internal order and state authority, the accommodation of the hundreds of thousands of Palestinian refugees who had found asylum there, and normalization of the situation on the Lebanese-Israeli border. Although the Lebanese had not taken part in the 1967 and 1973 wars and had suffered no territorial losses, Sarkis wanted Lebanon to participate in the Geneva negotiations and be a party to a general and definitive peace agreement that would replace the 1949 armistice agreement with Israel.

In Riyadh, King Khaled and Crown Prince Fahd voiced the same views I had heard in Cairo, Amman, Damascus, and Beirut. They, too, were in favour of a negotiated settlement in Geneva but thought it pointless to hold a conference if it was clear from the outset that it would lead nowhere.

Again and again, my Arab interlocutors pointed out that a solution was out of the question so long as the justified demands of the Palestinians were ignored. It would be a delusion, they said, to believe that the Palestinians would ever give up the idea of their own state. In that connection, President Sadat showed his understanding of Israel's fears regarding the founding of an independent Palestinian state and therefore suggested a close link between such a state and Jordan. His main concern was Israel's basic willingness to recognize the Palestinian nation. Such willingness, he believed, would create the prerequisite for a compromise solution.

All the Arab statesmen were agreed that it was unacceptable to exclude the Palestine Liberation Organization from the negotiations. They pointed out that the PLO was regarded as the only legal representative of the Palestinian people, not only by the whole Arab world but by the majority of all states. The Saudi Arabians, who placed particular value on United States mediation in the Middle East conflict, held the view that US influence would diminish considerably if Washington rejected all contact with the

PLO. Without exception, all felt that the PLO had to be represented in Geneva in some way or other.

Opinions on how the PLO might be included varied. King Hussein and President Sadat did not reject the possibility of a compromise formula providing for PLO inclusion in a joint Arab delegation. There was, however, unanimous insistence that the PLO should receive its own invitation to the conference, since that would confirm its right to speak on behalf of the Palestinian people.

I met with Yasser Arafat, leader of the PLO, during my stay in Damascus. The meeting had been arranged before my departure from New York, but for security reasons the time and place were kept open until the last minute. During our three-hour talk, Arafat frankly explained his standpoint. He stated that the PLO wanted the establishment of an independent Palestinian state. To achieve this goal his organization was, in principle, prepared to take part in any conference aimed at a solution of the Middle East conflict, but it would insist on being invited as an equal partner in the discussions. He would not commit himself on whether the PLO would accept such an invitation, saying that such decisions could only be made by the controlling body of the organization. Arafat stressed that the two Security Council resolutions – 242 and 338 – on whose basis the 1973 Geneva Conference had taken place made no mention of the national rights of the Palestinians and merely referred to the necessity of a solution to the 'refugee problem'. He said that it was difficult for the PLO to accept such a wording, especially since the United Nations General Assembly had recognized the Palestinians' right to self-determination. That reservation notwithstanding, he did not exclude the possibility of his organization's accepting an invitation to Geneva.

When the discussion came round to mutual recognition between Israel and the PLO, Arafat said that it was too early to talk about such things. Recognition of the State of Israel could only be considered at the end of negotiations. Arafat appeared to assess the situation realistically and repeatedly stressed his desire for a peaceful solution. As in all other conflicts, here, too, it seemed a matter of whittling down ideologically determined points of departure and reducing the emotional factors. Only then could any dialogue between those involved lead to the beginning of concrete peace negotiations.

I tried to explain this viewpoint to the Israeli leaders in Jerusalem during my visit in February 1977, but they showed no inclination to shift from their position. As Prime Minister Rabin explained to me in the presence of Foreign Minister Allon and Defence Minister Peres, Israel considered the PLO to be a terrorist organization threatening its security. They had no sympathy for the General Assembly resolutions by which the Palestinians' right to self-determination and the PLO as representative of the Palestinian people had been recognized. In their view, the Geneva Conference should be convened strictly on the basis of Security Council Resolutions 242 and 338, which did not specifically recognize the national rights of the Palestinians. As far as Arab representation at the conference was concerned, Israel rejected the idea of a joint Arab delegation but had no objection to Lebanon's participation.

Although they assured me that, like the Arabs, they were interested in setting a date for the Geneva Conference as quickly as possible, they did not consider it appropriate to convene the conference before the question of Palestinian representation had been clarified. Moreover, as Rabin explained to me, they wanted to know in advance whether the Arabs were thinking of a genuine peace agreement or merely ending the state of war.

I left the Middle East in February 1977 with mixed feelings. A greater readiness to compromise was certainly in the air. Yet I observed no real change on the essential questions, especially representation for the Palestinians. Still, the general view was that the time for progress towards a peaceful settlement in the Middle East problem had come. Never before had the desire for peace been so evident on all sides. A climate of moderation and common sense prevailed favourable to the efforts of the United Nations and of the co-chairmen of the Geneva Peace Conference. It seemed quite possible that the Geneva Conference would convene again in the second half of the year.

Menachem Begin's election as Prime Minister of Israel brought a new element into the situation. I have come to know Begin better since that time and respect his patriotism. I also believe that he is seriously concerned to find a peaceful solution to the Middle East conflict, which weighs so heavily upon his country. But the fact cannot be ignored that he feels bound to a set of principles which make negotiations for an over-all settlement and the search for compromise difficult; nor should it be forgotten that even before Begin's election there were great obstacles in the path to a second Geneva Conference, the major one being the question of representation for the Palestinians. Diplomatic efforts throughout the summer of 1977 were concentrated on overcoming those obstacles.

The United States played an important part in these efforts. President Carter and Secretary of State Cyrus Vance were both active in the search for a peace formula, but their initiatives were unsuccessful. Hopes that the conference could be convened before the end of the year suddenly dwindled.

In November 1977, President Sadat surprised the world by his unexpected decision to visit Jerusalem. That dramatic initiative was without doubt an event that will have prolonged psychological and political repercussions. Admittedly, it yielded spectacular results psychologically, but it did not bring about any immediate breakthrough at the bargaining table.

In later negotiations in Cairo, Ismailia, Jerusalem, and Washington, many of the same difficulties emerged on which earlier attempts at a solution had foundered. As far as the United Nations was concerned, the results of the Sadat initiative created some difficulty. All the parties involved in the Middle East conflict, including the PLO and both chairmen of the Geneva Peace

Conference, had been invited to what was known as the Cairo Conference, which was due to take place immediately after Sadat's trip to Israel. I had also been asked to attend. One cannot help wondering what would have happened if all had accepted. As it turned out, only Egypt, Israel, and the United States did. A number of Arab states voiced their misgivings; indeed, some had rejected the conference right from the start. Furthermore, one of the chairmen (the Soviet Union) had opposed both the Sadat initiative and the holding of the conference. In the end, the conference became a bilateral affair between Israel and Egypt in the presence of the United States. The majority of Arab States, including Jordan and Syria, followed its course with deep distrust.

Inasmuch as the prime obligation of the secretary-general is to support any effort towards a peaceful settlement of conflicts, I thought it would not be fitting to decline the invitation altogether. I therefore instructed the co-ordinator of the UN peace-keeping operations in the Middle East, General Siilasvuo, to attend the Cairo Conference as observer. At the same time, I considered it correct to state my own reservations. I suggested that at a later date a full conference with all those who had been invited to Cairo might be held on United Nations ground or somewhere acceptable to all. In that way we might at least discuss preparations for reconvening the Geneva Conference and establish whether or not the conditions for its success existed.

My suggestion got a mixed reception. The Arab states that had declined to go to Cairo reacted positively. The Israelis rejected it, although it had not been a formal proposal. I was concerned, as I explained at the time, to create a 'safety net' in order to offer all those concerned in the conflict (including Israel and Egypt) a foundation for negotiations on a broader basis, should the Cairo Conference fail. I still think that my suggested procedure might one day prove useful.

These events and the later pressure put on the United Nations to participate in further developments of the Egypt-Israel negotiations are good examples of the way in which the particular interests of member states can cause problems for the secretary-general. When difficulties arise, most states expect the Organization to give their standpoint credibility and prestige, especially if it is challenged by others. Certainly, as secretary-general, I must always offer my services in settling international differences. But, in doing so, I may not surrender my position as an impartial intermediary, nor can I allow having my office misused in any way – or my role as a universally acceptable and available third party is irreparably damaged. In the case of the Cairo Conference, I was criticized by both sides: by one because I was represented at all – even though only by an observer – at such controversial negotiations on the Middle East, and by the other because, in presenting my suggestions for the future, I had expressed reservations on the chances for success of the efforts in progress.

After prolonged negotiations, in which President Carter played a vital role, the Egyptian-Israeli treaty was finally concluded and came into force in April 1979. It was unquestionably a very important step in the apparently endless process of Middle East negotiation and secured the first major Israeli withdrawal since 1957, as well as being the first peace treaty between Israel and an Arab state. All the same, the achievement was greeted with scepticism in many quarters and with active, and even violent, opposition by a large majority of Arab states and the Palestinians. In particular, the 'general framework for peace in the Middle East', on which negotiations were to start within a month of ratification of the treaty, was violently attacked.

This situation leaves the United Nations, as usual, in the middle. We have to go on with the day-to-day measures – peace-keeping, communications, humanitarian efforts, and care of refugees – which, in the absence of real peace, keep the emotional, political, and military temperature in the Middle East at a workable level. We shall also have to be constantly alert for any opportunities to advance the progress of peace, knowing fully of the obstacles and frustrations that more than ever stand in the way.

At the same time that the Egyptian-Israeli treaty was being negotiated, other developments were taking place. Early in March 1978, the Palestinians had carried out an attack on Israel, during which more than thirty civilians had been killed. Although a strong Israeli retaliation was anticipated, its proportions surprised most observers. Israel launched a massive invasion of southern Lebanon. The use of fighter bombers and heavy artillery caused widespread damage. Some 200,000 people became refugees, but the Palestinian units, the primary target of the attack, managed to retreat to the north with most of their arms and ammunition.

During the deliberations of the Security Council on that difficult and explosive situation, the United States and the Western members strongly advocated sending UN troops into southern Lebanon, with the aim of confirming the withdrawal of Israeli troops, restoring peace, and ensuring the return of Lebanese government authority over the area. The Council accepted the proposal surprisingly quickly on Sunday, 19 March, and asked me to report within twenty-four hours on the positioning of a UN unit.

A UN Force in southern Lebanon was by no means a new idea; the proposal had been examined repeatedly over the preceding ten years. As a first step, we transferred one Iranian and one Swedish company from units serving the United Nations on the Golan Heights and in the Sinai Peninsula. As commander of the Lebanon operation I appointed General Erskine of Ghana, then chief of staff of the UN military observers in the Middle East; his observers were to form the preliminary staff of the operation. General Siilasvuo, chief co-ordinator of UN peace-keeping operations in the Middle East, was in turn given responsibility for contacting the governments concerned.

The French government immediately made troops available and within twenty-four hours put a French parachute battalion on stand-by. It took up its position within the week. Other troops were provided by Norway, Senegal, and Nepal. They were later followed by contingents from Ireland, Fiji, and Nigeria. From a technical standpoint, it was not difficult to get the troops to the area, but what caused me concern were the conditions, once they got there, the vague formulation of their mandate and the special problems inherent in the Lebanese situation.

The first problem arose from Israel's decision to extend the radius of its military activities beyond the original ten-kilometre-wide 'safety belt' to the Litani River, although not occupying the city of Tyre, which was held by a group of heavily armed commandos who were certainly not prepared to submit to UN control.

The second problem had been bothering us for some time, especially in relation to our military observers on the Israeli-Lebanese border. For many years, the Lebanese government had had no control over the area, various sectors of which were held by different armed groups – Christians, Palestinians and others – each dominating a number of small villages. It was a situation that created continual danger and difficulty for our men. Maronite Christians under the command of Major Haddad controlled the eastern region. In the west, Palestinian units and left-wing Lebanese movements were in control. In addition, a civil war had been smouldering in the area for several years, with all the factions being materially supported from the outside. In normal circumstances, UN peace-keeping forces operate on the territory of a sovereign state under some sort of functioning administration, a condition that did not exist in southern Lebanon. In other peace-keeping operations in the Middle East there had been a clear agreement between those concerned on the character, the functions, and the scope of the peace-keeping force, with each of the parties assuming certain obligations. Not so in southern Lebanon. The mandate of the Security Council merely commissioned the UN troops to confirm the withdrawal of Israeli forces, to establish peace in its area of operations, and to ensure that it was not used for hostile acts of any kind. Furthermore, the utmost effort was to be made to facilitate the restoration of the authority and sovereignty of the government of Lebanon in the area.

This was certainly not the first time that the secretary-general and the commanders in action had had to interpret an obscurely worded mandate from the Security Council. To make it even more confusing, there was no clear definition of the 'operation area', and each of the controlling groups had its own ideas about what the United Nations should and should not do.

In order to clarify the situation, I decided shortly after the Lebanon action had begun to visit the area for myself and discuss the many unresolved issues with the Lebanese government, with Arafat, and with the Israeli government. I also wanted to ascertain the problems of our soldiers at first hand and discuss them fully with Generals Siilasvuo and Erskine.

I arrived in Beirut on 17 April by special plane. I had lengthy discussions there with President Sarkis, Prime Minister El-Hoss, and Foreign Minister Boutros. The journey from the airport to the President's palace served as a perfect symbolic introduction to the difficulties facing the government. Instead of taking the direct route, we were driven to our destination under heavy secret escort via countless side roads.

My talks with President Sarkis and his colleagues centred primarily on the collaboration between the Lebanese government and the UN peace-keeping force that would be required to restore the sovereignty of Lebanon in the area between the Litani River and the Israeli border. Sarkis explained that there would be practical difficulties, primarily because of the virtual non-existence of a Lebanese army and inadequately trained administrative personnel.

Since sending Lebanese troops to the south was out of the question for the moment, President Sarkis proposed that additional units of the Lebanese gendarmerie be provided to assist our troops in carrying out their control duties and to serve as liaison with the local population. His government at that time was simply not capable of anything more. He did agree, however, to dispatch Lebanese troops to the area at a later date. I was already realizing how much effort and patience would be needed for a long time to come before normal conditions could be restored in the area we were supervising.

On the same day that I spoke with the Lebanese leaders, I was to have a meeting with Yasser Arafat at the headquarters of the United Nations Armistice Commission in Beirut. During luncheon with President Sarkis, I learned that Arafat had subsequently proposed that we meet at a secret place of his own choosing. Although I was warned how dangerous it was to go through the turmoil of Beirut to some unknown spot, I knew the meeting was necessary for our peace initiative and, in particular, for my mission. Even the former chief of general staff of Israel, General Gur, had indicated that he considered Arafat and his organization essential factors in the restoration of peace in southern Lebanon.

That afternoon we were called for by a PLO liaison officer, who drove on ahead in an old limousine, while we followed in another car. As he guided us through the streets of Beirut, amid considerable public excitement and uproar, we suddenly realized that our Lebanese police escort had left us and that several jeeps with young, heavily armed Palestinian irregulars had taken over our protection. The closer we got to our meeting place, the more armed Palestinians appeared in the streets; and when suddenly one of the young soldiers fired a burst from his submachine gun into the air, the tension heightened even more. By the time we arrived at Arafat's house, our escort had to force a path for us through the crowd.

In contrast to the uproar outside, the atmosphere in which our talk took place was calm. Arafat repeatedly stressed that he wanted to work with the United Nations to implement the Security Council resolutions. I left with the feeling that Arafat was genuinely desirous of co-operating with our troops.

That evening we flew from Beirut to Tel Aviv, where we

immediately met with Defence Minister Ezer Weizman. Weizman introduced me to the new Israeli chief of general staff, General Eytan, a tough and taciturn front-line soldier. Although Weizman stressed that Israel would like to withdraw its troops from southern Lebanon, he spelled out the reasons why it could not be done in the near future. I pointed out the risks arising from such a delay and warned of the outbreak of fresh hostilities, should the United Nations be prevented from implementing its resolutions. The primary condition for a successful UN action in southern Lebanon was the withdrawal of Israeli troops. We finally agreed that General Siilasvuo and General Eytan should discuss the details of the next phase of the Israeli withdrawal the following day.

In my talks with Prime Minister Begin and Foreign Minister Dayan, I learned that the Israelis had been impressed by the energy and self-assurance of the UN troops in southern Lebanon and, perhaps, even a little surprised. The talks developed in a friendly atmosphere, despite my insistence that withdrawal of the Israeli troops had to be carried out as quickly as possible, and before I left Israel a day later, I was given the plans for the next phase of the Israeli withdrawal.

I flew by UN helicopter directly from Jerusalem to Naqoura, the provisional headquarters of the UN troops in southern Lebanon. Naqoura, which had once been a Lebanese customs post and was at that moment still under Israeli occupation, had suffered badly in the recent fighting. The UN accommodation was in the open amid the ruins of the customs building fronting the sea. After a brief talk with the commander of the UN troops and his officers, we set off in convoy along the coastal road towards Tyre. As we left the Israeli-occupied zone, we passed a control post manned by French UN soldiers and shortly afterwards encountered a Palestinian road-block. At that point, things started to get critical. The crowds along the road thickened and became more excited as we approached the refugee camp of Rachideyeh, where a huge demonstration against the Israeli invasion and its use of cluster bombs was taking place. The empty containers of weapons had been set up in the middle of the road as gruesome evidence, and some demonstrators were brandishing undetonated grenades, which looked like green golf balls. The crowd became unruly, and some young men jumped onto our car, beat their fists on the roof and doors and tried to prevent us from driving on. Our column finally managed to get going again, and with some difficulty we reached the entrance to the Tyre barracks where the French parachutists were stationed. A large and violent demonstration was going on here as well.

When we had inspected the French unit and their quarters, we learned that the barracks were practically surrounded by demonstrators. Originally, we had planned to drive on to the port of Tyre, which was not under UN control but occupied by Palestinian irregulars and armed left-wing groups; but the situation was so threatening that we were taken directly by helicopter from the barracks to our next stop-off. All the same, it was an instructive and moving experience to have witnessed the bitter despair and the violence prevailing among the people of the region. It was also sobering to see the quality and quantity of the weapons with which almost all of the men and children lining the road were armed.

Our flight followed the coast from Tyre, over lemon groves and banana plantations, towards the highlands, which were intersected by deep, wooded valleys, an area over which UN control had been restored. Then we flew along the south bank of the Litani River and made our first stop in a hilly area where our Iranian contingent was positioned. From there, we went eastward to the Norwegian UN positions on the edge of Marjayoun, the headquarters of Major Haddad's Christian militia. Between these two landings we flew over a group of Major Haddad's soldiers.

Southern Lebanon is a beautiful country, but the geographical layout of the terrain makes effective control of infiltration extremely difficult for our troops. Since 13 June 1978, when the Israeli forces withdrew, we have been faced with a new and even more serious problem. The Israelis, instead of handing the southernmost strip of Lebanese territory over to the United Nations Force, handed it over to Major Haddad, whose Christian militia are supplied and supported by Israel. Haddad's forces have opposed any further deployment by UNIFIL in the southern zone and, backed by Israelis, maintain a hostile attitude, which they often emphasize with artillery fire. Haddad is particularly opposed to the deployment of the legitimate Lebanese army in the south, and serious incidents occurred when the first Lebanese battalion was sent into the UNIFIL area in April 1979.

It is a highly frustrating situation. The Lebanese government believes that the re-establishment of its authority in the south must begin with the deployment of its armed forces throughout the area, and they have already sent out one battalion. The Israelis believe that their security depends on maintaining the Haddad area as a 'safety belt', or security zone, as long as the PLO are still in force north of the Litani River. UNIFIL, therefore, is blocked from achieving one of its main objectives. It cannot use force, and, in my view, such a course of action would fundamentally alter the peace-keeping nature of its task. Moreover, to do so would probably lead to a confrontation not only with Haddad but with the Iseraeli forces. We must, of necessity, proceed by diplomacy and negotiation, and, at the moment, this is uphill work. On the other hand, I am convinced that the presence of UNIFIL, even in its current limited area of operations, is a major and vital contribution to peace in the Middle East. Should the UN Force be withdrawn for any reason, all of the combustible elements in the area would join in an enormous explosion that would certainly not be confined to southern Lebanon itself. As the situation now stands, I believe that we must maintain our Force in Lebanon while continuing to try to achieve all of its objectives.

In southern Lebanon we have excellent officers and soldiers from many countries whose determination, attitude and discipline deserve the highest respect. They are fully aware of the dangers of the job they are doing, which requires patience, restraint and diplomacy. Since they are barred from using their arms except for purposes of self-defence, their task is in many ways far more difficult than that of front-line soldiers. The casualties they have sustained are certainly proof of this.

The UN action in Lebanon is not only of extreme importance with regard to the tragedy of the Lebanese people in particular and to peace in the Middle East as a whole; it is also a test case where the readiness for action and the reputation of the United Nations have been put on the line. If the Organization manages to carry out this action successfully, the world will have more confidence in its ability to tackle other dangerous situations – that in southern Africa, for example. That is why it is of decisive importance for us to convince all the parties involved that their collaboration with the United Nations is the safest way for them into a better future. It is proving a long, complicated and arduous process, but I am convinced that it is the only serious method by which peace can eventually be achieved in southern Lebanon.

CHAPTER NINE

The Third World

AN INDIAN DIPLOMAT once told me that the area we call the Middle East was West Asia in the eyes of his countrymen. His remark took me by surprise. Like anyone else who has grown up in Europe or the Americas, I had learned at school to give the area the name which Westerners consider universally valid. But, actually, why should Middle East be more correct than West Asia? The question seems strange only to those who persist in thinking that Europe is the centre of the world and that everything has to be defined with reference to the West. They do not realize that over the last three or four decades our global concept has changed radically. What we now call the Third World – that large group of African, Asian and Latin American countries which eschews alignment with any of the major political systems of the world – has long been one of the essential components of the community of nations.

Three great statesmen can be credited with creating the concept of non-alignment that allows the Third World to express its own philosophy and main concerns forcefully and make itself heard. India's Prime Minister Nehru, President Nasser of Egypt, and President Tito of Yugoslavia were the leaders who had the necessary imagination and wisdom to realize that the less-developed countries had to join forces and, above all, remain independent of the military and political blocs resulting from the Cold War, if they were ever to make their influence felt in world politics.

Since the principle of non-alignment was first proclaimed at the 1955 Bandung Conference, it has become a fundamental reality of the international situation and is so universally accepted today that people tend to underestimate the great creative vision that produced it. Of its three early proponents, only President Tito is still among us. Because of the sympathy he has shown the Third World countries, the Yugoslav head of state is considered by many the pioneer of this dynamic movement. Marshal Tito, whom I have frequently met over the years, has always impressed me profoundly. Though he runs his country's affairs with authority and competence and plays a lively part in international politics, he is basically a man of simple tastes and pleasures. He spends his free time walking, swimming and working at various handicrafts. At his residence on the island of Brioni, where he receives visitors, he is a warm-hearted host, a connoisseur of good wine, and takes great delight in being able to offer his guest vintages he has grown himself.

The newly independent nations today not only constitute the majority in the international community but are also demanding that they be given their rightful place and treated as equals. They are getting increasingly impatient with the egocentricity of the West, which, as far as they are concerned, bespeaks a lack of understanding and fosters prejudice.

In Western circles, however, it is not uncommon to hear that independence has proved a mixed blessing for the new nations. It is also sometimes pointed out that most Third World states are governed by dictatorial régimes. Quite apart from the fact that such comments at the diplomatic level scarcely contribute to the improvement of relations between the industrialized and less-developed countries, they demonstrate a serious want of logic. Such thinking stems from the mistaken premise that Western democracy is not merely the best form of government but the only one – and, therefore, automatically valid for all peoples, regardless of their culture, history, and standard of living. We have a tendency to forget the long and often bitter events that preceded the evolution of national unity and democracy in the countries of

Europe. Some Third World nations have tried to adopt Western democracy, in most cases without success. It is not a system which can function in a social order based on tribal principles or among groups that have not achieved even a minimum of national cohesion. Too often we forget that in many Third World countries independent forms of self-determination have evolved over the centuries that are better suited to the traditions of their peoples.

There is also the accusation that fundamental human and civil rights are violated in many Third World countries. Regrettably, such violations do exist, and it is our duty to do everything to eliminate them. But we should also recognize that violations of human rights are not restricted to the Third World.

In order to rationalize the slow development of the Third World countries, some Western critics cast doubts on the capabilities or integrity of their leaders. As a generalization, such criticism can hardly be justified. The government representatives of young states whom I have known are certainly as qualified as their colleagues from the developed countries with respect to education, culture, and efficiency in office. And no country or group of countries has a monopoly on corruption. Its practitioners in the industrialized nations do not even have the excuse of poverty.

Underdevelopment, often the cause of human suffering and death, is one of the basic problems of our time. It seems to me inexcusable that in this period of great scientific and technical progress, this time of unparalleled abundance in most industrialized countries, more than a quarter of the world's population remains undernourished and hunger is a daily condition for broad sections of our world.

The problems of the Third World have been blamed on the population explosion and the resulting imbalance between the number of people and the resources available to them. In fact, it is underdevelopment itself that is at fault. This is why many governments give such priority to the eradication of illiteracy and the establishment of training and other educational programmes.

In my countless trips to Africa and Asia, I have witnessed the enormous efforts being devoted to these objectives.

Since population, resources, environment, and development are recognized to be interrelated, the question whether it will be necessary to institutionalize birth control is profoundly important. The World Population Conference, held in Bucharest in 1974, offered no clear answer. The 137 countries represented not only professed quite divergent outlooks but also differed on the expediency and means to be used for family planning. Nevertheless, the conference was useful in that it brought to light various factors affecting the formulation of any policy on birth control. Some participants – Catholic and Muslim – emphatically defended the right to life on the basis of religious principles. Others were opposed to birth control for economic and even political or military reasons. Another argument was that a higher living standard served as the most important factor in checking the population explosion. Several delegates recalled that among very poor, mainly rural families, children were regarded as a profitable investment, since they could be thrust into the work force at the earliest possible age. The diversity of views expressed revealed the complexity and delicacy of the problem. Nevertheless, some basic principles were formulated: the sovereignty of each state concerning population policies; respect for human life; recognition of the family as the basis for society; and the right of married couples to decide on the size of their family. It was also reaffirmed that those governments that wished to reduce the rate of population growth in their countries should benefit from greater international aid.

One particularly interesting development at the conference was the insistence of some Third World countries, supported by the socialist states, on a more equitable distribution of goods through the creatiton of a new international economic order. Failing that, they explained, the problems of underdevelopment, including overpopulation, could only be solved by radical measures.

There are weighty arguments in favour of a new order for the world economy. It is not right that the 70 per cent of the world's population, which produces a large proportion of the raw materials, should have to subsist on only 30 per cent of the world's available income. The situation is all the more unfair in that roughly one hundred of the poorest countries are in danger of becoming poorer in relative terms, and certain of these poorer in absolute terms. Even now, in twenty-four such countries, the people are on the verge of starvation, since their average annual per capita income is less than $200. The rising cost of energy, food and industrial products, and the drop in prices for raw materials all serve to aggravate the economic crises in these countries.

It can be argued, of course, that this situation is a logical consequence of the law of supply and demand. But it is precisely this *laissez-faire* carry-over of nineteenth-century liberalism that the less-developed countries reject as a system that functions only in favour of the industrialized states. The country whose economy is essentially dependent on a single commodity – say, its copper deposits or cocoa harvest – risks disaster if the price of that commodity suffers a severe drop. Industrialized nations, having achieved a certain economic equilibrium through broad diversification of production, are largely immune from such hazards.

The proportion of the national income of the industrialized countries made available to the developing countries in the form of development aid is dwindling. The external debt of the less-developed countries increased fourfold from 1962 to 1972 and is now somewhere around $200 billion.

Of course, the developed countries voluntarily finance various assistance programmes, such as the United Nations Development Programme, which has an annual budget of more than $500 million, and the emergency relief programmes, especially those concerned with food distribution, all of which mainly benefit the poorest nations. In 1973, the industrialized states of the world pledged themselves to make available at least 0.7 per cent of their gross national income for development assistance. To date, however, most of them have fallen short of that quota, and the amount of foreign aid that is received scarcely corresponds with the capacities of the donors. In 1976, the total spent for development projects was only $19 billion, though armaments expenditures exceeded $400 billion. In 1976, only $5 billion was raised for agricultural assistance to the Third World, where 430 million people suffer from protein deficiency—no more than 1.75 per cent of all military expenditure that year.

Neither money nor labour is sufficient to secure the development of a national economy. The Third World urgently needs assistance in technological development, a sector in which the newly independent countries are particularly deficient and the support of the industrialized countries leaves much to be desired. With respect to technological resources, developing countries, with few exceptions, see themselves in a situation of total dependence, lacking the freedom of choice that is indispensable for the exercise of national sovereignty. One often hears the phrase 'neocolonialism of the computer'.

The problem of development is neither purely economic nor purely political. At the 1976 United Nations Conference on Trade and Development in Nairobi, I pointed out that political decolonization must be followed by economic decolonization and that only by fruitful co-operation would it be possible for the poor and the rich nations to achieve a more equitable status. I stressed that this new phase would be decisive for the future of mankind, 'a liberation movement in the truest sense of the word aimed at liberating the masses of humanity from poverty, hunger, unemployment, and despair'.

The emancipation movement of the Third World nations showed its first sign of life immediately after World War II, long before the decolonization wave of the 1960s. In January 1952, the United Nations had officially recognized the right of developing countries to control their own natural resources. Six years later, a commission was set up to study the question of realizing that right.

In 1962, a UN resolution reinforced the principle of the permanent sovereignty of states over their natural resources. The first UN Conference on Trade and Development, held from 23 March to 16 June 1964, marked an important step in the long struggle of the Third World towards full emancipation. Its major contribution was the elaboration of a definition for a new economic policy, the essential objective being to restructure the prevailing international economic order, which was recognized as manifestly unjust for two thirds of the world. The conference tackled the question of reforming international trade, not only with respect to existing regulations but, above all, through the promulgation of quantitative and long-term projections. In that context, measures were also worked out for overcoming the chronic deficit in the trade balance of the less-developed countries.

Parallel to the actions taken by the United Nations, and in conjunction with them, there has been great expansion of the non-alignment movement. Twenty-five countries were represented at the summit meeting of non-aligned states in Belgrade in 1961; at the 1964 Cairo Conference, the number had risen to forty-seven; and in 1970, fifty-four Third World states met in Lusaka. The high point of this movement, so far, has been the Colombo Conference of 1976, which was attended by the heads of state and representatives of eighty-four Third World countries. The most significant conference of non-aligned states, however, was that held in Algiers in 1973, at which the participants requested the UN secretary-general to convene, at the highest political level, a special session of the General Assembly to deal with development questions and renovation of the structures of the world economic order.

At the special session, which was convened six months later, the UN membership declared its readiness 'to work urgently for the establishment of a new international economic order based on equity, sovereign equality, interdependence, common interest and co-operation among all states, irrespective of their economic and social systems'. For the first time in its history, the General Assembly devoted itself exclusively to development problems. For three weeks, ways of closing the gap between the industrialized nations and the less-developed countries were debated. As I stressed at the time, this would be the greatest challenge for our Organization since its foundation.

On 1 May 1974, despite a number of reservations on the part of the industrialized nations, the Assembly adopted two extremely significant resolutions, setting forth the Declaration on the Establishment of a New International Economic Order and a programme of action for the realization of the new order. In that declaration, the right of a state to nationalization of its natural resources and economic activities is defined as 'the expression of the full, permanent sovereignty of the state', and sovereignty over its own natural resources and means of production is held to be the indispensable precondition for the independence of a developing country. 'No state', the General Assembly declared, 'may be subjected to economic, political, or any other type of coercion to prevent the free and full exercise of this inalienable right.' The Assembly also recognized that the increase in costs of imports – particularly foodstuffs, energy, fertilizers and industrial equipment – had steadily increased the existing burden of external debt for many poor countries. It called upon the developed countries to increase their aid to those countries and intensify their investments in industrial projects; furthermore, they should consider cancelling the external debt of the least-developed countries or, at the very least, apply moratoria on long-term refinancing.

That special session of the General Assembly, the sixth in its entire history, was the first real step towards the creation of a new international economic order. The details were worked out a year later, in September 1975, at the Assembly's seventh special session. In twenty-two plenary sessions, lasting more than ten days, the relevant measures were discussed by representatives of both the developed and the developing countries, openly and in a spirit of readiness to understand one another's problems, and the existing differences were classified. The Third World nations expressed their desire for greater control over the future of their economy and a fair share of the world's prosperity. The industrialized countries explained their concern with regard to guarantees for the continuing supply of energy, raw materials, and other products at suitable prices. All the participants recognized that, in the common interest, a new era of co-operation must come into being.

The talks essentially took place between the representatives of the Third World and the Western states. The socialist states of Eastern Europe were less fully involved; they supported the basic arguments put forth by the developing countries but they were not, in fact, directly concerned. Actually, 75 per cent of the trade of the developing countries is with the OECD countries; a further 20 per cent is taken up by trade among the developing nations themselves; and only 5 per cent involved trade with the socialist states.

The seventh special session ended on 16 September with a unanimous resolution consisting of seven chapters concerning questions of international trade; monetary reform; the establishment and strengthening of scientific and technical infrastructures in less-developed countries; industrialization; nutrition and agriculture; and co-operation among the Third World countries themselves. The resolutions also contained proposals for a restructuring of other economic and social sectors of the international system.

That comprehensive document might appear dull to laymen; yet its content was of capital importance for the future of mankind. As the result of a compromise at the global level, an action programme for all spheres of daily life affecting the well-being of hundreds of millions of people in poor as well as rich countries had been worked out. The recommendations, taken as a whole, had led mankind to a crossroads. The remaining question was whether the world community would be courageous enough to follow through.

Three months after the seventh special session of the General

Assembly, the Conference on International Economic Co-operation was convened in Paris. What came to be known as the 'North-South dialogue' between representatives of the industrialized nations and the Third World countries lasted for eighteen months. The conference did not fulfil expectations. In the end, the industrialized nations were not yet ready to accept the fundamental change in the world economic order that the Third World countries insisted was the sole solution to their development problems.

Comprehensive changes do not come about instantaneously. A new climate must first be established. In the final analysis, such changes influence every individual, so it is imperative that the public be informed of the processes and decisions that go into their making. That is why international conferences fulfil an extremely important explanatory role, even if they do not always produce concrete results. Only within the framework of a world-wide organization like the United Nations can global questions of such magnitude as reformation of the world economic order be dealt with. Some might object that the United Nations is too cumbersome an apparatus for sustaining a permanent North-South dialogue. I cannot agree. It is not a matter of organizational considerations but of political will. That concrete and effective solutions are possible is proved by the creation, in 1967, of the International Fund for Agricultural Development, for which more than $1 billion was made available by the industrialized countries and the members of OPEC. Apart from its immediate importance, that success also signalled the first fruits of efforts to create a new international economic order.

The true reasons for the present stalemate in the North-South negotiations are a matter of political objectives; for their part, the industrialized countries are still too firmly attached to their past and fearful of radical change. The Third World, on the other hand, does not always appreciate the internal difficulties of the industrialized nations and the true causes for Western hesitations. In my opinion, it is a matter of creating a new relationship of trust between the developed and the developing countries. A better understanding of each other's historical, cultural, and political situations must be induced in order to lead the dialogue to success. Since I myself come from a country that for years was under foreign domination, I feel great sympathy for oppressed peoples. And, as I have already indicated, I was raised in an environment where tolerance was not just an empty phrase. Since my first contacts with the United Nations in 1955, I have always listened with the fullest attention to what Third World representatives say about the problems and hardships of their peoples. My many journeys in those countries have given me some insight into what is happening there and evoked that inner compassion which is necessary for true recognition of problems and for bringing them closer to solution.

Aside from moral considerations, there are also some purely practical aspects of the development question which I think will lead to compromise. The industrialized countries obviously cannot do without the raw materials available in the Third World countries; nor can the Third World countries do without the technology, equipment, or products indispensable for progress today. Moreover, the industrialized countries are currently facing economic problems they cannot solve by themselves. Problems such as inflation, unemployment, and competitive marketing must be solved on a global basis, and this requires partnership with the less-developed countries. In particular, it will be necessary to give the developing nations the chance to become equal trading partners. Because many less-developed countries are economically dependent on a few raw materials, production of these will have to be given priority. In order to stabilize the current broad fluctuations in the prices of such raw materials, efforts within the framework of the United Nations led to the decision to create a fund for the formation of buffer stocks. In common with other measures, this could prove an essential contribution to strengthening the position of the Third World nations as trading partners and encouraging both sides to more fruitful co-operation.

Both sides are aware of this need, even though they may hold conflicting views. The fact remains, however, that those countries which lack the barest necessities can no longer wait. They have struggled for decades so that the United Nations Charter might be valid for them too. The developed countries are under relatively less pressure; but they, too, admit that the present economic system is no longer tenable. Moreover, they are aware that in many sectors, particularly the monetary, its inflationary and other negative effects work to their disadvantage. Their reactions to the demands of the Third World are prompted by a certain anxiety; but, as I have frequently pointed out, it is not a question of destroying the economic system of the industrialized states but rather of developing new structures that would serve the long-term interests of all.

Both time and patience are needed. Still, no problem is solved by ignoring it or shelving it. And caution is not in every case the mother of wisdom. Clearly, without co-operation on economic problems, stabilization of political relations among nations must remain an illusion.

I fully realize that the governments of the West are confronted with serious domestic problems. They have not always been capable of preparing public opinion in their countries for the changes that have taken place in the world. The economic crisis, inflation, the drop in purchasing power, and unemployment are often obstacles opposing measures that would benefit the Third World. A new economic order cannot come about overnight. But if there is no progress, only confrontation remains, which would have long-term catastrophic consequences for us all. Fortunately, all countries are becoming increasingly aware of this danger. I am therefore confident that the necessary solutions will be found.

CHAPTER TEN

Into the Future

IN THE FOREGOING PAGES I have tried to give my impression, within the bounds of discretion imposed by my office, of the job of the secretary-general and the activities of the United Nations. I have described the frustrations as well as the satisfactions of the task, the bright as well as the dark side of the World Organization, and the reasons why I believe it to be indispensable. Regardless of the difficulties, the disappointments and the never-ending stress and fatigue the job involves, I consider it the highest possible privilege to serve as secretary-general. As I said in the General Assembly on the occasion of my re-election in 1976: 'The post of secretary-general is at the same time one of the most fascinating and one of the most frustrating jobs in the world, encompassing, as it does, the height of human aspiration and the depth of human frailty.'

The United Nations, like all human institutions, is far from perfect, and we who work in it know its imperfections as well as or better than anyone. But we also know its present value to the governments and peoples of the world and the unique promise it holds for the future. To maintain international peace and to build a better world order are immensely ambitious tasks. Those who undertake them must be determined and dedicated. They must be ready for all kinds of difficulties and frustrations, but they must also be fundamentally optimistic. The United Nations was founded on the belief that the human race is capable, by an effort of will, of improving its lot and fulfilling in a more satisfactory way its promise and its genius. Unless one believes this, the work of the United Nations has little or no meaning. If one does believe it, however, as I most firmly do, no work in the world could be more rewarding.

Although sometimes the difficulties seem overwhelming, it is encouraging to see how much the United Nations has achieved in its first thirty-four years of existence and how it has responded to, and in some cases acted as a catalyst in, the tumultuous changes that have occurred in this unique period of history. The world of 1979 is radically different from the world of 1945, and the Organization has also radically changed. With three times its original membership, it is active in a variety of new fields scarcely dreamed of by its founders. Admittedly, its plans and objectives are sometimes more impressive than its practical performance, but that is not unusual for human institutions, especially one reflecting a new world in the process of active evolution. As Dag Hammarskjöld once remarked, 'The United Nations reflects both aspiration and a falling short of aspiration, but the constant struggle to close the gap between aspiration and performance now, as always, makes the difference between civilization and chaos.' The struggle to close the gap has widened and diversified since Hammarskjöld's time, but the task and the rationale remain the same.

Underlying all of the activities of the United Nations is the problem of balancing and reconciling national sovereignty and interests with international responsibilities and the long-term interests of the world community as a whole. Within this basic task, one can discern three main threads in the work of the Organization. The first of these is the maintenance of international peace and security, without which all other tasks would soon become meaningless. The short-comings of the United Nations are nowhere clearer than in its efforts to maintain the peace, and nowhere are the reasons for them more manifest.

The Organization can only achieve what its sovereign members wish it, or are willing to allow it, to achieve. With their assent and co-operation it can do much to forestall conflict, to put an end to violence, or to contain a threatening situation while a settlement is being sought. On countless occasions, the Security Council has provided the means and the pretext to retreat from a dangerous confrontation. In times of crisis, when a conflict threatens to escalate and to involve even the greatest powers, the Council has many times shown its vital importance as a place of last resort and as an alternative to full-scale war. It has also been successful in formulating basic guidelines for the settlement of many complex disputes. It has improvised the technique of peace-keeping as a practical method of containing conflict.

The Security Council, however, can only perform its task effectively if governments are willing to avail themselves of its assistance, respect its decisions, and co-operate with it. If they are not prepared to bring a problem to the Council, the United Nations can be of little help. Or if, as is all too often the case, governments ignore a decision of the Council because it does not happen to suit their immediate purposes, it is extremely difficult, if not impossible, for the Council – or the secretary-general, for that matter – to implement its decisions. The side-tracking or ignoring of the Security Council erodes its prestige and weakens its position as a keystone of the system of world order set forth in the Charter. As I have said on many occasions, I regard this as potentially one of the most dangerous trends in the history of the United Nations. None the less, I believe that the over-all work of the Security Council has been of inestimable value in maintaining peace and in preventing the escalation of local conflicts into world-wide conflagration.

The second main thread in the work of the United Nations is its function as an agent of peaceful change. From its inception, the Organization has played a crucial role in the great movement of decolonization. I have no doubt that without the United Nations this process would have been far more bloody and disruptive, far more difficult for the former colonial powers, as well as for the newly independent nations, and, certainly, far more protracted. On the political side, the original mechanism of peace-keeping has played an important role in maintaining quiet during periods of transition and, on occasion, in filling the power vacuum created by the withdrawal of the old colonial powers.

We are now facing an even more fascinating stage in the management of change – the effort to adjust the relationships of developed and developing nations in the new world that has evolved since World War II. In fact, this effort (the so-called North-South dialogue) has, to some extent, replaced the East-West problem as the dominating theme of UN activity. We see this adjustment taking place in the political work of the Organization, above all in efforts to tackle the global problems that have arisen from technological change and the growing interdependence of nations, and in the current efforts to establish a new international economic order. Such an objective would have been inconceivable ten years ago, and, even now, the task is infinitely complex and the obstacles extremely daunting. But I believe that it says much for the vitality of the Organization and the vision of its members that a task of such magnitude can be seriously considered and pursued. The readjustment of the economic relationships of all nations and groups of nations in the world is an immense challenge. I do not believe that it could be undertaken anywhere else than in the United Nations, with its nearly universal membership.

The third main thread in the world of the United Nations is the attempt to plan in advance, on a co-operative global level, for the future. As in all political organizations, those who work in the United Nations are usually fully occupied with the problems and concerns of the present. We must not, however, allow these pressing and immediate duties to exclude a vision of the future. Indeed, I believe it is esential to have such a vision constantly in mind if we are to maintain any equilibrium or sense of direction in the turbulent and confusing world in which we live. Each task we undertake, each response to a particular situation, should not only fulfil its immediate purpose but should, if possible, carry us a step further towards a more reliable, equitable, and just world order.

I do not believe that a world government will suddenly and miraculously come into existence and be accepted by all nations. I do believe, however, that we can and must evolve a better system for managing the affairs of the world through the give-and-take of debate, through facing dangers together, through learning to co-operate and through the development of an overwhelmingly strong sense of common interest. We know perfectly well that there are already a number of areas – disarmament, the environment and energy, for example – where we must co-operate or face the greatest risks of chaos and decline, if not destruction. No task of the United Nations is more important than the steady expansion of the area of common interest among nations and the provision of acceptable means by which governments will voluntarily limit their sovereign rights in the long-term common interest. This has been achieved on a large scale with individual rights in most national societies. We now have to accomplish the same in the community of nations. That is the meaning of much of the arduous, long, not always stimulating, and sometimes acrimonious work of the various bodies of the United Nations system. Given the political and psychological realities of our time, I do not believe that there is, at present, any realistic alternative to this complicated, seemingly endless, and often frustrating search for a better future world order.

We should not, I think, be unduly discouraged at the rate of progress. Rome was not built in a day, and the objectives we are pursuing are immensely ambitious and, for the most part, have never before been attempted. If we look back, we can see that much has already been achieved. Concepts that would have been unheard of in 1945 are now universally accepted. Although there are still periods of recrimination, the level and content of the dialogue is impressive and wide-ranging. If national sovereignty and national interest are still the primary motivations of governments, there is an increasing willingness to discuss increased international responsibility and control as the indispensable framework of an interdependent world. And I am sure that governments are now better informed, partly because of the United Nations, of one another's positions and hopes and fears.

If we can continue to avoid the disaster of world war, we should be able to build steadily a structure of world order that will make the earth a more agreeable and a safer place for all of its inhabitants. It is an immense task and, inevitably, a slow one, but the United Nations is available as a unique mechanism for this purpose, if only its members will use it.

The vision of the future that I try to keep in mind is a world where governments and peoples will learn to work together and to unite their strength for great common purposes. It will be a world of better understanding, less prejudice, and less futile, and often dangerous, wrangling. It will be a world where reason and co-operation will be signs of strength rather than of weakness, a world which makes a virtue of interdependence while maintaining the glories of diversity and freedom. It will be a world of peace in which men and women can pay more attention to developing their creative instincts and their capacity for free expression within a framework of benevolent order.

I do not believe that such a vision is naïve or illusory. Seven years as secretary-general provides a stringent lesson in realism and in the weakness, as well as the strength, of human nature. Certainly, my vision of the world will not be realized in my lifetime, but I see no reason why it should not come about within a measurable span of years. And, after all, the possible alternatives are unbearable.

In my experience nothing is less realistic than cynicism or defeatism, and nothing more enduring than a practical and determined idealism. The aims and principles of the Charter were the product of the greatest and most disastrous war in history. They were the ideas of men who had looked into hell and were determined that future generations should not be forced to do the same. They were realistic, battle-tried, experienced men. I see no reason, after thirty-four years of comparative peace, to doubt the validity of their ideas and ideals or to conclude that their vision of a world peace and justice is unattainable just because the difficulties are so great.

I do not expect miracles or spectacular successes. Sound political progress is seldom based on either. But I am convinced that the United Nations provides the best road to the future for those who have confidence in our capacity to shape our own fate on this planet.

APPENDICES

APPENDIX ONE

Preamble to the Charter of the United Nations

WE THE PEOPLES OF THE UNITED NATIONS DETERMINED

to save succeeding generations from the scourge of war, which twice in our lifetime has brought untold sorrow to mankind, and

to reaffirm faith in fundamental human rights, in the dignity and worth of the human person, in the equal rights of men and women and of nations large and small, and

to establish conditions under which justice and respect for the obligations arising from treaties and other sources of international law can be maintained, and

to promote social progress and better standards of life in larger freedom,

AND FOR THESE ENDS

to practise tolerance and live together in peace with one another as good neighbours, and

to unite our strength to maintain international peace and security, and

to ensure, by the acceptance of principles and the institution of methods, that armed force shall not be used, save in the common interest, and

to employ international machinery for the promotion of the economic and social advancement of all peoples,

HAVE RESOLVED TO COMBINE OUR EFFORTS TO ACCOMPLISH THESE AIMS

Accordingly, our respective Governments, through representatives assembled in the city of San Francisco, who have exhibited their full powers found to be in good and due form, have agreed to the present Charter of the United Nations and do hereby establish an international organization to be known as the United Nations.

APPENDIX TWO

Report of the Secretary-General on the Work of the Organization

Submitted to the General Assembly at its Thirty-fourth Session
September 1979

I

THE PAST YEAR has been full of uncertainty, tension and conflict. The international scene has never been more complex nor the old concepts of power so diffused. There have been sudden shifts in the political balance and unexpected developments rooted in a variety of forces – economic, political, social and even religious. There is an increasing uneasiness as to the manageability of the affairs, and especially the economic life and social organization, of the planet in the circumstances now prevailing. These uncertainties and unforeseen developments affect in different ways the lives and the future of virtually all nations and peoples and give rise to deep-seated feelings of anxiety and frustration, which in turn create a climate favourable to new and unpredictable events.

If ever there was a time for serious reflection and stocktaking on the state and future of the community of nations, it is now. In our current anxiety we have, to some extent, lost sight of the enormous advances that have been made on so many fronts in the past 30 years. What we now require is the necessary spirit of accommodation to take full advantage of those advances.

In the upheavals of our time we can discern certain general trends – the desire to remedy long-standing injustices or ancient grievances, the compulsion of national aspirations, anxiety over the possibility of a viable future for this or that nation, the fear of the designs and ambitions of others and the suffering, frustration and resentment caused by gross economic and social inequities. A generation of unprecedented change has inevitably left many unresolved problems, old and new, as well as a sense of disillusionment at the failure to realize many of the great aims and objectives proclaimed in the optimistic aftermath of the Second World War.

Most of the symptoms and problems I have mentioned are ones which the United Nations, if effectively utilized as the working structure of the world community of the future, could be of unique assistance in solving. We need, above all, to press on with the development of the elements of such a community on a global basis. This is not a matter of abstract idealism but of practical self-interest. It is also a matter of urgency.

There are a number of obvious reasons why the development of an effective world community will be difficult and slow. At one end of the scale we have the complex relationships of the greatest Powers, which are still to a considerable extent prisoners of their mutual fears and suspicions and of the fearful destructive capacity of their weapons systems.

At the other end of the scale the majority of nations and peoples are afflicted in varying degrees by acute problems of instability, poverty and economic weakness, often exacerbated by political and economic developments elsewhere in the world. While the aspirations of their peoples are high, economic dependence or instability shackles many of them to an economic system which no longer meets the requirements of an interdependent world of free nations. For many of them their first generation of independence has coincided with the challenge of coming to terms with a new world, a world in a state of revolutionary technological change. Thus the general longing for peace and equity is shadowed by a widespread unease and lack of confidence in the future.

Between these two poles, many middle and smaller Powers, within the United Nations and in various groupings outside it, have steadily developed a sense of co-operative responsibility on many global issues. The non-aligned movement is a good example of this positive trend. In the United Nations they have shown by and large a mixture of idealism and pragmatism which constitutes a most constructive middle force in the affairs of the world. This, in my view, is one of our best hopes and assets for the future, particularly at a time when the polarization of the world situation caused by great Power tensions would appear to be becoming a less dominant factor of the international scene as other independent political, economic and social forces emerge.

The great Powers have special responsibilities and obligations in the United Nations system. They also have a special need for the world Organization as an alternative to the kind of confrontation which, in our nuclear age, could well be fatal to us all. The United Nations, and especially the Security Council, has played a vital, if unappreciated, role for many years in providing alternatives to such a confrontation. In recent years the major Powers have on a number of occasions availed themselves of this moderating mechanism during periods of crisis. The United Nations has also played an invaluable role in insulating regional crises to the necessary extent from the delicate balance of nuclear Power relationships. This is certainly not the comprehensive system for the maintenance of international peace and security envisioned in the Charter of the United Nations but in the extraordinary and, it is to be hoped, transitional conditions of our world, it represents an indispensable safeguard of world peace and survival.

Elsewhere, the United Nations, through the process of decolonization, through its pioneering activities in development, in its current search for a new international economic order and in an increasingly broad attempt to tackle global problems, has been, and is, the centre of an effort to find new arrangements fitting and adequate for our interdependent world. The objective of such arrangements should be above all to try to make the fundamental changes necessary to lessen the gap between rich and poor and open the door of opportunity to all. The problems and obstacles are uniquely complex and difficult, and progress is slow, but the focus and the objectives are there. Later in this report I shall revert in more detail to this central and essential part of our task.

It cannot be said that the past year has witnessed any striking progress on our main problems. Indeed, the lack of progress, especially on the economic side, is distinctly disappointing and in strong contrast to the evident urgency of most of the problems. Political determination and a sense of pragmatism are necessary to reverse this debilitating situation.

II

Adjustment to change is inevitably a difficult and long process, and we should not overlook what has already been achieved during the life of the United Nations. Indeed many of the developments which we now take for granted or complain about as inadequate would have seemed quite out of reach only a few years ago. What we are trying to create in the United Nations is a world order fundamentally different from any that existed before. This is no small task, and we must remind ourselves from time to time of how much has already been achieved, as well as of the formidable obstacles that remain.

In the relationships of the most powerful nations, for example, much has been done to temper the adverse climate which coloured so strongly the post-war years. In spite of ideological, political and other differences, accommodations have been reached which certainly contribute to making the world a safer and more productive place. We need only think, for example, of the positive development in the relations of China and the United States. This year, we should remember the conclusion, after most complex negotiations between the United States and the USSR of the SALT II agreement which offers hope of limiting the growth of strategic nuclear weapons, an indispensable prerequisite to progress on the general problem of disarmament.

The process of accommodation is vital to progress on the various acute regional problems which preoccupy the United Nations. International instruments are essential and useful only if their possibilities are utilized for achieving the accommodations – sometimes quite small in themselves – which could make enormous contributions to world stability.

I have been increasingly aware of the need to encourage by all means the kind of adjustments which could remove, or at least alleviate, the various regional tensions which are still, in my view, the most dangerous threats to world peace. It is mainly for this reason that I have travelled extensively in order to get a first-hand view of such problems and to discuss them directly with the Governments concerned. Very often, of course, little can be achieved in the existing political circumstances but, if a channel of communications or good offices can be of help, I feel strongly that the Secretary-General should be available. In any case there is no substitute for getting to know the problems on the spot and at first hand.

It was with this end in view that I undertook, earlier this year, an extensive tour of East Asian countries. During this trip I had especially the Indo-Chinese and Korean situations in mind, and I very much hope that our talks in the various capitals may provide a basis on which the Governments and parties concerned may feel more ready to reconsider their positions and to use the possibilities the United Nations offers to assist them in solving their problems.

The United Nations has been especially preoccupied this year with developments in Indo-China – developments which not only raise fundamental questions of Charter principles but also have been accompanied by vast and tragic humanitarian problems. Naturally these matters were predominant in the discussions I had during my visit to the region. The concern of the international community has, throughout this year, been focused both on the political and military developments in Indo-China and on their humanitarian consequences. It has seemed to me that, at the level of human tragedy now prevailing in that part of the world, humanitarian concerns must be attended to without delay.

This view is in no sense intended to downgrade the importance of a political settlement in the area. The situation which has followed the long and cruel war in Indo-China not only threatens the peace and stability of South-East Asia, it could very well also become a threat to world peace. It is of the utmost importance that the process of adjustment start at once and be carried on in a constructive and forward-looking spirit by all parties. As I have already informed them, I am ready to provide any assistance which the Governments concerned may think useful or desirable.

In this as in other situations that have recently arisen, it is imperative that all efforts be directed towards finding a settlement in conformity with the principles of the Charter of the United Nations, in particular respect for the territorial integrity and political independence of all States, non-interference in internal affairs and the non-use of force.

III

Of the great political problems for which the Organization has specific responsibilities, the Middle East continues to be the most urgent and complex. There can be no doubt that this question is central to the political, economic and military stability of the world. As long as uncertainty, discord, frustration and violence prevail in the Middle East, the world will continue to live with a profoundly destabilizing element in its affairs and with a grave and continuing risk of future disaster.

The Middle East problem is so sensitive that it is virtually impossible to make any suggestions or proposals about it without upsetting some, or sometimes all, of the parties concerned. This sensitivity has been faced by the succession of mediators, representatives, negotiators and good offices missions that have tried to be of assistance in the last 32 years. The question is how long the world, let alone the peoples of the Middle East, can afford to go on living with this explosive issue in its midst.

The dramatic developments which led to the conclusion of a peace treaty between Egypt and Israel have created a new situation in the area. It is a measure of the complexities of the Middle East problem that this event has given rise to controversy and division. Once again, understanding and far-sightedness, while maintaining principles and vital interests, are essential in what would otherwise be a hopeless situation. It is now more than ever necessary that all of the parties concerned review their position with the future rather than the past in mind.

A just and lasting peace in the Middle East can ultimately only be achieved through a comprehensive settlement covering all aspects of the question including in particular the inalienable rights of the Palestinian people. Evidently, all parties concerned must be involved. I believe that the United Nations, if used with imagination and forebearance, offers in this regard unique possibilities which have not yet been fully utilized, and I hope that these possibilities will be more seriously examined in the coming months. For example, as I have previously suggested, an international conference, properly prepared, might well provide a way out of the present dangerous situation. Evidently a serious process of consultation with all of the parties will have to precede such an international meeting.

In the meantime, the practical involvement of the United Nations has continued to be mainly in the field of peace-keeping – the unceasing effort to keep down the temperature and to avert the confrontations which could so easily lead to widespread conflict and make all movement towards peace impossible. I shall revert later in this report to the subject of peace-keeping operations.

I must, however, mention here the situation in southern Lebanon. The most explosive elements of the Middle East situation exist in close proximity in and around southern Lebanon and their interaction represents both a national tragedy for Lebanon and a constant threat to the wider peace. In recent weeks there has been a serious escalation of violence in this area, resulting in civilian casualties, heavy damage and the flight of many inhabitants. After repeated efforts, an uneasy cease-fire is in effect at the time of writing. This tragic and volatile situation is a reflection of the wider problems of the region and will not be finally resolved until solid progress on those problems is made. In the meantime, we shall continue our efforts through the United Nations representatives in the area, and especially the Commander of the United Nations Interim Force in Lebanon (UNIFIL), to maintain the present relative calm. The situation in this troubled and tragic area has been for many years a vicious circle of violence and reprisal in which the perennial losers have been the civilian population. I appeal to all concerned to co-operate with UNIFIL and to show restraint in maintaining a cessation of firing and hostilities pending the time when a more radical improvement in the situation is possible.

Developments have been disappointing in Zimbabwe and Namibia, for which the United Nations has a special concern. The difficulty in resolving the question of Zimbabwe and the now critical situation in that territory are causes for grave anxiety. An enduring solution of this problem can only be assured if there exists a constitution which has the agreement and support of all parties concerned. The internal settlement as well as the elections held under it do not meet this requirement and cannot, therefore, be recognized as forming a basis for genuine majority rule. Renewed efforts must be made to bring all the parties together to co-operate on an acceptable and lasting settlement. Unless this can be done soon, there is a serious danger that all the progress made on this question will be lost in bloodshed, disorder and ruin with serious implications for the security of the whole region. I hope very much that the ideas and plans which emerged from the recent Commonwealth Conference at Lusaka may provide the means of achieving such a settlement. Meanwhile, it is important that all Member States adhere to the measures called for by the Security Council and work together in resolving this problem.

A year ago there seemed good reason to expect an early solution to the problem of Namibia on the basis of the plan of action approved by the Security Council. Unfortunately, the establishment of a United Nations presence in Namibia to supervise and control elections has been delayed. The full co-operation of all concerned is essential to the implementation of the Security Council's plan of action. Although difficulties have arisen over the interpretation of certain provisions of the plan, I hope that current talks will result in the necessary clarifications so that we can proceed, with the co-operation of all concerned, to practical action. After so much effort has been made, it would indeed be regrettable if we were unable to achieve the final adjustments necessary for success.

The present state of affairs in Namibia and Zimbabwe has serious implications for the security and economic future of the whole region; involving, as it does, continued loss of life in those countries as well as large-scale raids into Angola, Botswana, Mozambique and Zambia, with resulting casualties and widespread destruction. It is absolutely vital that means be found to make practical progress on these two problems without sacrificing the principles laid down by the United Nations.

Our aim should be the stable and prosperous future of southern Africa as a whole. This will not be achieved, however, as long as the problem of apartheid persists. One of the great challenges confronting the United Nations and all the peoples of the region is the absolute necessity of transforming the racial situation in southern Africa so that men and women of different races can coexist and exercise their rights as equals.

Another area of conflict with which the United Nations has been intimately involved, both in its peace-keeping and its peace-making roles, is Cyprus. The United Nations Peace-Keeping Force in Cyprus (UNFICYP), which has been there for more than 15 years, continues to perform an indispensable function in maintaining calm in the island. At the same time, I have pursued the good offices mission entrusted to me by the Security Council to promote a just and lasting settlement. To this end, I convened a high-level meeting at Nicosia last May under my personal auspices. That meeting resulted in a 10-point agreement calling for the resumption of the intercommunal talks and setting forth the basis and priorities for them. While the talks were resumed amid high hopes, they soon encountered difficulties which necessitated an early recess. I have instructed my representatives to continue our efforts to overcome the difficulties in the way of restarting the talks in accordance with last May's high-level accord and the priorities established in that agreement.

The present situation in this regard comprises two sets of difficulties. One concerns the stated negotiating positions of the parties. The other relates to political problems that they face in tackling the compromises and accommodations that are essential if the talks are to have any meaning. Time and again it has proved possible to bridge important differences between the parties and to agree on guidelines and priorities that held out the prospect of progress towards a settlement. Time and again the momentum generated by these agreements has been allowed to dissipate. Moreover, the existing *status quo* tends to create a dynamic of its own, which does not necessarily facilitate an agreed solution. It seems to me, however, that a far-sighted and determined approach, based on the existing guidelines and accords, could lead to a rapid improvement of the situation in the island that would serve the interests of all concerned and would be vastly preferable to continuing to cling to an unsatisfactory and potentially unstable *status quo*. This could at the same time clear the way for a comprehensive political settlement, based on the fundamental and legitimate rights of the two communities and on the right of all Cypriots to a better and more peaceful future.

IV

The United Nations now have five peace-keeping operations in the field. A sixth operation, the United Nations Emergency Force (UNEF), has recently lapsed, and much thought and effort have been devoted to a prospective operation in Namibia, the United Nations Transition Assistance Group (UNTAG).

These operations are interrelated both by their basic nature and by the fact that the success and credibility of existing operations have an effect on the acceptability and chances of success of future peace-keeping efforts, since confidence is an essential element of successful peace-keeping. Peace-keeping is one of the original creations of the United Nations and is a valuable instrument in the Security Council's efforts to control conflict and maintain international peace and security. It is a delicate and complex mechanism which can only function properly if certain basic conditions exist and if all concerned are prepared to give it their full support and co-operation. Otherwise, peace-keeping operations can become controversial and even self-defeating, with a consequent decline in the confidence of Member States in this very useful and innovative technique.

Peace-keeping operations tend to be set up in the heat of the moment to defuse a crisis and contain a conflict which may otherwise spread or seriously upset the fragile balance of world peace. The resolutions which initiate these operations set goals which are sometimes not easily achievable in reality. A prolonged failure to achieve such objectives tends to generate a mood of frustration which, in the long-run, may even jeopardize the future of the operation itself, regardless of the service it has rendered or is rendering in controlling a conflict. This in turn is discouraging to the troops in the field, to the Governments which provide them and to the members of the Security Council which set up the operation in the first place.

A fundamental prerequisite of successful peace-keeping operations is the co-operation of the parties concerned. If one or other of these opposes, or has strong reservations about, the objectives of the operation, it is unlikely to be completely succesful and will in all probability become an additional source of controversy and friction. The problem then arises whether the actual value of the operation in terms of maintaining peace justifies its continuation in the face of opposition. This is a crucial question which should be considered on its merits and with utmost seriousness by all concerned.

When a peace-keeping operation is firmly based on a detailed agreement between the parties in conflict and they are prepared to abide by that agreement, it is relatively easy to maintain. This has been the case, for example, with UNEF and the United Nations Disengagement Observer Force (UNDOF). When, however, an operation is mounted in an emergency with ambiguous or controversial objectives and terms of reference, and on assumptions which are not wholly realistic, it is likely to present far greater difficulties. This is undoubtedly the case with UNIFIL.

I am firmly convinced that UNIFIL has performed, and is performing, an absolutely essential task of conflict control in one of the most sensitive and explosive parts of the world. This seems to me to be an overriding argument for maintaining it in spite of all difficulties and disagreements. While I shall persist in my efforts to achieve the objectives set for UNIFIL by the Security Council, I think it is important that the current value of the operation, in all its difficulty, should be more fully recognized. The easiest way to prove the value of the task UNIFIL is now performing would be to withdraw the Force. In the present circumstances this would undoubtedly be a highly irresponsible and almost certainly disastrous experiment, and I do not believe that anyone properly informed of the situation would seriously advocate it.

This being the case, I hope we shall have the continuing support and understanding of Member States, the parties concerned and, indeed, the media in the very difficult period which UNIFIL is now experiencing. The Force was put into southern Lebanon precisely because the situation there was dangerous, complex and not susceptible of any obvious or easy solution. While searching for the way to a resolution of the basic problems involved, we should resist the temptation to ascribe them to the operation which is gallantly trying to keep the situation under control.

The United Nations Emergency Force, the mandate of which lapsed on 24 July, had served for nearly six years. It was set up urgently in a time of intense international tension and was deployed in a confused and still violent conflict situation. It was remarkably successful in stabilizing the cease-fire and implementing successive disengagement agreements. It has assisted the transition from conditions of war to a peace treaty in its area of operations. The Force has been an outstanding peace-keeping operation. I take this opportunity to express warm appreciation to the commanders, officers and men and to the civilian component of the Force for their dedicated and effective service to the United Nations.

The future United Nations role in the former UNEF area is still not clear at the time this report is being written. The military observers of the United Nations Truce Supervision Organization in Palestine (UNTSO) have meanwhile remained in the area under existing decisions of the Security Council.

While in no way detracting from the importance and excellent service of later and larger peace-keeping operations, I wish to take this opportunity to pay tribute to the observers of UNTSO, this oldest of United Nations peace-keeping missions which has operated continuously in the Middle East for more than 31 years, often in conflict conditions. Established originally in 1948 to supervise the first truce called for by the Security Council in the Middle East, UNTSO has carried out over the years a variety of peace-keeping tasks entrusted to it by the Security Council in the light of the changing circumstances in the region. Its dedicated officers from 17 countries have long since established a universally accepted reputation for objective and accurate reporting even in the most dangerous circumstances. They have assisted in de-escalating innumerable incidents, in arranging cease-fires, in performing countless tasks of a humanitarian nature and in providing a vital and unique link between parties in conflict. They have provided the initial framework and staff upon which all the successive peace-keeping forces in the region have been founded and have assisted these forces in performing their various tasks. They have suffered serious casualties in carrying out their essential but little-publicized work. They continue to be an invaluable resource for peace in the Middle East. The United Nations owes a debt of gratitude to this international group of courageous officers.

The United Nations Peace-Keeping Force in Cyprus has been stationed in the island since 1964 and has performed invaluable services in maintaining peace in a deeply troubled area. After the events of 1974 the role of UNFICYP changed fundamentally, but until now its continued presence has been considered essential to maintaining peace and the necessary atmosphere for negotiations on a settlement of the Cyprus problem. While the need to maintain peaceful conditions in the island is undiminished, the intercommunal negotiations have been making very slow progress and, as of the writing of this report, are in recess. The experience of UNFICYP raises in an acute manner the question of the relationship between peace-keeping and peace-making functions of the United Nations. The risks involved in the premature withdrawal of a peace-keeping force are well known and can scarcely be envisaged at this time in regard to UNFICYP. However, the time may soon come for a careful re-examination of the United Nations arrangements in the island in the light of present realities.

Peace-keeping is an invaluable addition to the armoury of peace. It is still, however, to some extent in an evolutionary stage and must be used with great care and attention to the fundamental principles and conditions involved. If this is done, I have no doubt that it will develop into an increasingly consistent and dependable support for international peace and security.

V

During the past year, the world continued to face increasing economic difficulties. In almost every area, economic problems multiplied. Many countries experienced unacceptable levels of inflation and unemployment. Exchange rates have been unstable and volatile. Protectionism has increased. Foreign trade has stagnated. Economic growth has been slow and errative in industrialized countries. The developing countries have found it impossible to finance reasonable rates of development. Official development assistance has stagnated at about half the target figure agreed in the International Development Strategy. The situation is becoming critical, and a continuation of present trends would seriously jeopardize the pace of development in developing countries for years to come. This in turn would reduce growth and prosperity in the industrialized countries. The forces at work in the world economy call for strong co-ordinated action to remove the structural causes of the present difficulties.

Under these circumstances, it is regrettable that there is a growing disparity between urgent economic problems and the inadequate responses by the international community. The ongoing mulilateral negotiations have so far failed to achieve results commensurate with the magnitude of the needs.

There has been some movement during the past year – the recent trade negotiations undertaken by the parties to the General Agreement on Tariffs and Trade (GATT), the agreement on the fundamental elements of a common fund for commodities, and the enlargement of quotas and the increase in special drawing rights in September 1978. These steps, welcome as they are, fall far short of what is needed. The GATT agreements provide a framework for the fight against future protectionism but give little immediate relief for countries most affected by present protectionist measures. Much more needs to be done to establish the common fund and to implement the other components of the Integrated Programme for Commodities. The enlarged quotas and the new special drawing rights are clearly inadequate to deal with the increasing balance-of-payments deficits and accumulated foreign debt of developing countries.

The fifth session of the United Nations Conference on Trade and Development was the first occasion on which an international conference specifically focused on the subject of structural change. The results were limited and disappointing. That session showed clearly that many countries were still reluctant to accept the full implications of growing interdependence in the world economy.

The multilateral negotiations now taking place within the framework of the United Nations are clearly facing difficulties. The Committee of the Whole established under General Asembly Resolution 32/174 adopted two sets of agreed conclusions. One dealt with the transfer of resources and one with agriculture and food issues. Although these constituted limited progress, the Committee has not succeeded in providing impetus to other negotiations within the United Nations system. The Preparatory Committee for the New

International Development Strategy made no progress in its first sessions in drafting the Strategy.

In the face of obviously pressing economic needs, such slow progress in negotiations is unacceptable. It is essential that all States should take urgent heed of the dangers of delay and reassess their positions in the light of their long-term interests and needs.

A new impetus in North-South negotiations would do much to dispel the present climate of uncertainty and disenchantment. This new impetus can only be found by a real political will to reach solutions. The United Nations is well equipped with machinery for intergovernmental discussions, consultations and negotiations. It has the capacity to support negotiations if Member States are prepared to use it with determination to find solutions to the problems besetting economic development.

Political support needs to be mobilized if acceptable solutions are to be reached. Brief high-level meetings could play an essential role in this process. Such meetings could also identify possibilities for agreement and priorities for negotiations. Naturally I stand ready to lend all necessary assistance in furthering such an approach. There are, in addition, other important areas for urgent international co-operation. Two of these have recently been highlighted by the World Conference on Agrarian Reform and Rural Development and the United Nations Conference on Science and Technology for Development.

The energy problem has emerged as a central and immediate concern for all nations. The progressive exhaustion of known cheap supplies of oil, while energy demands continue to increase, poses a formidable challenge for the international community. It also has profound political implications. Nations will need to change from a pattern of energy consumption dominated by oil to a more energy-saving pattern of growth, relying on more diversified sources of energy. If this transition is to take place in an orderly way, without putting undue strains on the world economy, intensive co-operation among States will be necessary. In addition, considerable efforts will be needed within each State. Planning and co-ordination will be required to harmonize the interests of producers, processors, users, poorer consumers and environmentalists and to achieve an equitable distribution of the burden of necessary adjustments, nationally and internationally.

In recent times, I have been intensifying my contacts with Governments on the question of energy to investigate their perception of the problem and to determine what initiative might be taken within the United Nations in this area. From these contacts I sense a growing recognition that in the future the question of energy should be a priority issue in the North-South dialogue.

Given the interdependence of the problems of the world economy, energy cannot be treated in isolation from other issues. Energy is particularly closely connected to international financial and monetary questions such as reserve creation, payments financing and development assistance. The time has come for the United Nations to work towards a balanced and integrated set of agreements and understandings in these areas. In doing so, we must find ways to ensure sustainable supplies of energy for the world economy while avoiding the excessive depletion of natural resources at the global and at national levels, and remaining consistent with the right of countries to exercise permanent sovereignty over their natural resources.

Determined action by the international community is thus required in three areas:

- We need to organize our efforts to bring the negotiations on the implementation of the new international economic order out of their present state of stalemate;
- We need to deal vigorously with the area of energy, which is a major challenge, and to launch a co-ordinated and imaginative effort by the world community in this field;
- We need to address the urgent problems of the oil-importing developing countries in a concerted and effective way.

It is my firm conviction that the United Nations is the place where all these efforts could be combined.

VI

The Third United Nations Conference on the Law of the Sea, at the end of its eighth session this summer, approved a programme of work providing for the adoption of a convention on the law of the sea next year. Although some isues have yet to be solved, the delegations attending the Conference unanimously agreed that it was possible, as a result of the many sessions of informal negotiations, to adopt formally a draft convention during the spring and act upon it during the summer with the aim of adopting a convention before the end of August 1980.

The long-sought convention can now become a reality if all the States participating in this, the longest and most comprehensive diplomatic conference ever convened under the auspices of the United Nations, make a last effort to achieve mutual accommodation on the few remaining issues. Many questions that appeared intractable when the Conference began its work almost six years ago seem to have found solutions that States can accept in a spirit of compromise.

Vital principles and interests are at stake, and the outcome of this Conference could greatly influence the willingness of Governments to make full use of the machinery of the United Nations to achieve international understanding on global issues. I hope, therefore that in the final stages of the Conference, Governments, having made remarkable progress on this most difficult and complex of issues, will find it possible to reach the necessary accommodations to produce a treaty which will be of fundamental importance for the future.

VII

The past year has witnessed some advances in the cause of the promotion and encouragement of respect for human rights and fundamental freedoms, but discouraging and grave new problems have also emerged.

While the world community has focused greater attention on human rights violations and has advanced in its recognition of the need to strengthen mechanisms for the protection of the individual, the number of instances of overt assaults on human dignity, sometimes on a massive scale, remains cause for deep anxiety.

Great hopes have been placed in the United Nations by peoples, persons and groups throughout the world which rightly expect the Organization to react in the face of the disregard or violation of human rights. We must realize, of course, that the United Nations has not always been in a position fully to meet these expectations. As I have pointed out in the past, the effectiveness of the United Nations in matters of human rights is inextricably linked with the attitudes of its Member States. It is the responsibility of each Member of the United Nations under the Charter to ensure respect for human rights within its jurisdiction; indeed the provisions of the International Bill of Human Rights are addressed essentially to Governments.

At the same time, the United Nations as an institution has important human rights responsibilities of its own to discharge under the Charter and under procedures and methods established by the appropriate deliberative organs. These include the setting up of internationally recognized standards for the protection and observance of human rights, marshalling the influence of the international community and of public opinion in support of such standards, monitoring the discharge of certain obligations assumed by Member States in this regard, and in certain cases inquiring into and drawing attention to instances of gross violations. In some instances, the United Nations has been able to act in unison despite the sensitivity of the issues involved. However, much remains to be done. The United Nations can realize its full potential in this field only when Member States face up to their responsibilities, as well as accept and live up to the trust which is placed upon them.

Among the more positive developments during the past year has been the wide-ranging debate on ways and means of improving the effectiveness of the United Nations in the field of human rights which took place in the General Assembly, in the Commission on Human Rights and in the Economic and Social Council. This debate is to continue in the future. For my own part, I am prepared to consider all useful suggestions for strengthening the contribution of the Secretariat in a field which is of fundamental importance to the future development of our society. Efforts have continued to be made in international organs which deal with human rights to instil a greater awareness of the relevance of human rights to development. The Commission on Human Rights has been considering an important study on the international dimensions of the right to development and has now requested further studies on the regional and national dimensions of this fundamental right. The Sub-Commission on Prevention of Discrimination and Protection of Minorities has also been considering the relationship between human rights and the new international economic order. Emerging from these studies is a recognition that there is a human right to development, that respect for human rights can create a climate in which people are inspired to greater efforts for development, and that human rights considerations must feature as essential components in the integrated approach to development.

Significant decisions have been taken during the past year by United Nations organs in dealing with situations of gross violation of human rights. Investigations have been initiated in some cases, individual experts have been designated to look into others, and in some instances I have been requested to undertake contacts with Governments with a view to discussing the human rights situations in their respective countries. The international community still tends to approach this delicate problem with caution in view of the other aspects of intergovernmental relationships which are often involved. For obvious reasons non-governmental organizations can afford to be, and are, much more forthright in their approach. I understand the reasons for governmental caution, reasons which also apply to some extent to the possibilities of the Secretary-General in many human rights cases. It is absolutely essential, however, that a cautious approach should not be allowed to degenerate into expediency on so vital a matter of principle.

Advances continue to be made towards the universal ratification of the International Covenants on Human Rights. However, the rate of ratification or accession needs to be stepped up if the goal of universality is to be attained without a long delay. In the Human Rights Committee, established under the International Covenant on Civil and Political Rights, Governments engage in a dialogue with the Committee in which their political, economic and social systems are subjected to international scrutiny from the point of view of their compliance with international human rights laws. The Economic and Social Council has also been working on the procedure for considering reports from States parties to the International Covenant on Economic, Social and Cultural Rights.

The United Nations continues to further and encourage regional, national and local activities for the promotion and protection of human rights, and has sponsored world-wide and regional seminars on these topics in the past year. An important step in the strengthening of regional human rights machinery has been the appointment by the Organization of American States of a newly-constituted Inter-American Court of Human Rights. The Seminar now taking place at Monrovia on the advisability of establishing an African regional commission on human rights is another encouraging step towards the strengthening of regional human rights machinery.

In the International Year of the Child, we have been reminded very forcefully of the stark deprivations suffered by children in many parts of the world and we have seen that all too often children are also victims of violations of human rights. It is absolutely intolerable that children should be made to suffer in this manner in our day and age. I earnestly hope that this and other objectives of the Declaration of the Rights of the Child will be furthered by the outstanding efforts which Governments and non-governmental organizations have made this year to promote the interests and rights of children all over the world.

For my own part, I have continued to exert my best endeavours on behalf of human rights whenever I consider that my actions may be of assistance to the persons or groups concerned. I am more convinced than ever that respect for human rights and fundamental freedoms must be at the heart of our greatest task here at the United Nations, which is to build a just and equitable world community for the future.

VIII

One of the agonies of the human condition has been the uprooting of millions of people from their homes and families to face unknown dangers, want and despair. To alleviate this appalling tide of human suffering, the United Nations has been deeply and increasingly engaged on behalf of refugees throughout the world.

Two important meetings were convened this year to deal with the problem of refugees. One was held at Arusha, United Republic of Tanzania, in regard to the refugee situation in Africa, the other at Geneva, on the problems of the refugees and displaced persons of South-East Asia. Both had positive results.

The Arusha Conference reaffirmed the principle that the granting of asylum is a peaceful and humanitarian act which should not be regarded as unfriendly by any State. It also stressed the importance of the scrupulous observance of the principle of *non-refoulement*. These principles are as pertinent in other situations resulting in the exodus of refugees as they are in Africa.

For the Indo-Chinese refugees, the United Nations High Commissioner for Refugees has conducted an operation of growing dimensions. As the exodus of Vietnamese, Lao and Kampuchean refugees continued to increase, however, and the countries of first asylum found the consequences so unbearable that they felt compelled to drive new refugees away, it became apparent that an even larger and more dramatic effort was required. The spectre of men, women and children drifting on crowded boats and often drowning, and of others on land, abandoned amid conflict, anarchy and famine, aroused the conscience of Governments and peoples in every quarter of the globe.

For these reasons, in consultation with the United Nations High Commissioner for Refugees and a number of concerned Governments, I decided to convene a meeting at a high level to deal with this humanitarian emergency.

I much appreciated the response of Member States to this initiative and their co-operation during the meeting. I am grateful to the many who made specific commitments of additional assistance to the refugee programme and to the related measures which were agreed on to reduce the dimensions of the problem and the tragic loss of life which had attended the unregulated and massive exodus that had been taking place. Offers of resettlement opportunities doubled from 125,000 to 260,000, and most substantial new pledges in cash and kind, exceeding $160 million, were received. The participants were, I believe as gratified as I was that so much could be accomplished in a two-day meeting of this kind.

In this undertaking, the essential objective was to meet immediate humanitarian needs. This in no sense detracts from the vital necessity of acceptable political solutions. It is essential that all concerned try to advance from the present stage of recrimination and conflict to a statesmanlike and far-sighted effort to resolve the underlying problems of this tragic and war-torn area. In the meantime, urgent steps must be taken to preserve the lives of the Indo-Chinese refugees and displaced persons and of the ravaged Kampuchean population. This must be done despite the political complexities, of which we are all aware.

IX

Like all political institutions in this age of change, the United Nations must face the problem of the manageability and suitability of its organization and procedures for confronting effectively the immense and pressing problems of our time. While I believe that most representatives shared the apprehensions in this respect expressed in my report on the work of the Organization last year, and more or less agreed with my analysis of the problem, very little seems to have changed in the intervening 12 months. In fact, in some respects things have become worse. To take one practical example, documentation; the situation is now such that the existing United Nations services can no longer carry the steadily increasing load. This threatened breakdown of a service which Member States more or less take for granted is symptomatic of the strain imposed on the international system by the steady inflation of activity and the lack of effective review and restraint.

I have been left in no doubt that many Governments of Member States are increasingly concerned at the drain on financial and personnel resources entailed in the continuing upward spiral of international meetings and related activities. It is apparently widely believed that action by the Secretariat could significantly diminish this trend. I wish therefore to state with all possible emphasis that the current and continuing proliferation of activities is directly attributable to the decisions of Member States in the various organs of the United Nations. These decisions, sometimes taken in an unco-ordinated and even casual way, create new institutions, new demands for documentation and services and generally add to the workload of services which have not been commensurately expanded. There is often, I may add, a wide discrepancy between such decisions of Governments and the views expressed by their representatives in the intergovernmental organs dealing with administrative and budgetary questions.

We must be realistic in trying to deal with this institutional inflation, which is not a new phenomenon nor one unique to the United Nations. We have to recognize that political considerations play a dominant role in organization and that the United Nations system, for better or for worse, is no exception to this rule. We have to accept that a perfectly logical and functional institutional system is probably not within our reach and that we must make the existing one function better. We also have to accept a certain degree of institutional escapism as the Governments of the world grapple with new and overwhelming problems. By this I mean that it is sometimes easier to call a conference, or even to found a new institution, than to confront a complex problem directly.

Within these limits, we must renew our efforts to rationalize our institutions, to make them more effective for their stated purposes, to direct and co-ordinate their activities for the maximum cumulative effect and to make them as responsive as possible to the real problems of our time. I and the Director-General for Development and International Economic Co-operation, together with our colleagues in the Secretariat and in the specialized agencies, will continue our efforts towards these ends. But these efforts cannot be effective without the active co-operation and understanding of the States members of the organizations concerned.

In an effort to improve the working methods of the General Assembly, I presented to the membership in June this year a report on the rationalization of the procedures and organization of the Assembly. Recognizing that a major modification of existing practices and procedures would require careful deliberation and lengthy negotiation among the Members, I have advanced a series of relatively modest proposals for improving the Assembly's work which will, I hope, command substantial support at the very beginning of the thirty-fourth session. The general objective of these proposals is to overcome some of the difficulties of coping, within the original time-frame allocated 34 years ago to the General Assembly session, with a workload involving four times as many items and three times the membership which existed when the United Nations was founded. I would hope that these proposals are only a beginning and that Member States will wish to continue the process of improvement with more radical steps.

The Geneva meeting on Indo-China refugees, which I have already mentioned in its humanitarian context, may provide some ideas for future efforts to cope with pressing problems on a basis different from the more traditional conference approach. With the full co-operation of Member States and in spite of the different political preoccupations of many of them, we were able to hold a short, business-like meeting devoted to a single primary purpose. The practical results of this meeting attest both to the spirit in which the participants came to it and to the usefulness of the method. I shall welcome suggestions from Member States as to other major problems which they feel might be dealt with through *ad hoc* meetings of this kind.

X

The capacity of an organization to deal effectively with its business and to be seen to have a useful impact is an essential basis for public confidence. In the United Nations, this simple maxim is complicated by the immense diversity of the public involved, and by the scale and complexity of the problems dealt with.

I feel obliged to say frankly that I continue to be disturbed by prevailing public attitudes to the United Nations and by our apparent inability to generate the kind of broad public support, confidence and understanding without which we shall not achieve the great objectives upon which mankind's future prosperity – even survival – may depend. It is true that there are moments, usually moments of international crisis and apprehension, when the potential of the Organization is realized and its usefulness in maintaining international peace and security is widely understood. It is true that there are many countries, especially in the developing world, where the assistance and the great programmes of the United Nations system in the economic and social field are appreciated and regarded as essential guides to the future. It is true that Governments faced with insoluble or unbearable problems do bring them to the appropriate organ of the United Nations in order to get help and share the burden. All of these reactions are important signs of what the United Nations can and should usefully do.

What has not so far been adequately developed is a general and consistent support of the aims and activities of the United Nations as a whole, as a working model for a genuine world community. This is particularly obvious in the response, or lack of it, to many of the decisions of the Security Council. It is clear also in the reluctance of many Governments to bring to the United Nations problems which obviously fall under the terms of the Charter until there is no other alternative and the problems have become too explosive and dangerous to ignore.

This lack of consistent support for the world Organization, created by Governments in 1945 to save succeeding generations from the scourge of war, may not seem to be of too great account in normal times, although it certainly means that the United Nations cannot always adequately perform the functions it was set up to perform. There is, however, a very real danger of losing precious time in acquiring what all agree is needed – the habit and experience necessary to make our world work in the new and highly complex circumstances of the 1980s. More dangerous still is the ever-present possibility that we shall be confronted, for a variety of expected and unexpected reasons, with a dramatic threat to international peace and security which the United Nations, in its present stage of development, may not be able to deal with.

These two considerations seem to me the most cogent reasons for renewing our efforts to gain widespread confidence and support among the peoples of the world. It is necessary to convince people that the struggle for peace, justice, equity and human dignity which is waged here at the United Nations is very much their struggle, and that their support, understanding and, if necessary, criticism, can make a real difference to the outcome. We shall not be able to do this by information programmes alone. We shall need, on important issues above all, to be able to show that the world Organization can, and does, treat them on their merits; that it can, and does, produce results which, however imperfect, constitute the difference between order and chaos, or even, in extreme circumstances, between peace and destruction.

This is a challenge which all of us have to accept if we are seriously to live up to the responsibility and the privilege of working in one way or another for the United Nations. If we can increasingly live up to this challenge, we should also be in a better position to ask that the media report more comprehensively and positively on our work in all of its aspects.

Public attitudes to the work of the United Nations range from strong support, through a mixture of lack of interest, boredom and even contempt, to active hostility in a few cases. Some of these attitudes can be explained by special circumstances. Others can only be explained by a failure to communicate and to convince. There is very little general understanding of the United Nations as a political institution, or as a system of specialized organizations, evolving in the new complexities and cross-currents of the contemporary world. There is almost no general knowledge of its capacity or importance as a balancing factor, a safety-valve or in conflict control. As the memories of the Second World War fade, there seems to be less and less comprehension of the necessity of building step by step, the framework of a working world community capable of withstanding the storms and facing the common problems of an uncertain future. Instead, small, and more or less irrelevant, matters tend to figure large in the popular image of the world Organization.

It is this situation which needs to be changed if we are to proceed from more or less abstract discussion to the phase of realization which at every step will require solid popular support. I hope that all Governments of Member States will consider this fundamental requirement of their Organization. I hope they will help us in the Secretariat, as well as all the voluntary organizations which are willing and anxious to be of assistance, to build the public support and confidence required if we are to make the United Nations increasingly effective.

In this connection, I am pleased to note that at its last session the General Assembly reaffirmed the necessity to foster in world opinion better knowledge of the aims and achievements of the United Nations, including the principles and purposes of the new international economic order. The Assembly requested me to take the necessary measures to ensure the close collaboration of Member States, the specialized agencies, non-governmental organizations and other information bodies in framing public information policies and programmes of the United Nations system. The Assembly also established a Committee to Review United Nations Public Information Policies and Activities, consisting of 41 Member States.

In the light of the constructive and helpful debate which has taken place this year in the Committee, as well as in its *Ad Hoc* Working Group, I look forward to receiving the general guidelines within which new directions for United Nations information activities may be sought and practical measures taken with a view to widening public support for the Organization.

XI

In my last annual report I stated that the concept of international civil service is at the heart of efforts to build an effective system of world order. For that reason especially, I believe that Member States should keep this basic issue constantly in mind. I have to say frankly that in my view the international civil service is at present at a critical juncture. Underlying this situation is the fact that an increasing number of Member States seem less willing to observe, in practice, the obligations they assumed under the Charter with respect to the independent nature of the Secretariat. This trend is frustrating in the sense that if a State or group of States does not honour these obligations, other States tend to follow suit for fear of losing their stake in the Secretariat. These developments put at risk the noble and essential experiment outlined in the Charter of building a truly international Secretariat working together with a common purpose for the United Nations.

In the previous years I have commented on the attitudes and

actions required to ensure the achievement of an effective, stable and independent international civil service. The full co-operation and understanding of Governments in this process is still not forthcoming, and I believe that there is an urgent need to re-evaluate our positions and attitudes towards the international civil service in the full knowledge that there are differing views on the matter. It will not be in the interests of the international community or of the Member States if the realization of the concept of an independent international civil service is so frustrated that it becomes more difficult to recruit, on a broad geographical basis, the highly competent and dedicated men and women we need to serve the cause of peace.

I mentioned the divergent views held by Member States concerning the very concept of an international civil service. It is evident that changes are taking place around us which have altered some of the basic professional requirements of the service. These changes have also affected the attitudes and commitment of staff members with respect to the Secretariat. We are in the process of trying to come to terms with these factors which, if neglected, will only weaken the international civil service. We are in particular making efforts to improve the situation with respect to the position of women and the role of developing countries.

Obviously it will take time to resolve these and other basic problems. During this process it is essential to strengthen our commitment to the principles and the objectives of the Charter on this question. The evolution of an effective international civil service is essential to the future usefulness of the United Nations in all its diverse fields of activity. Provided we have the commitment of the Member States to this goal and their understanding of the problems involved, we should be in a position to make significant progress on this fundamental problem.

XII

In keeping with the commitment I made during the thirty-third session of the General Assembly, I have pursued a determined policy of budgetary constraint which is reflected in the significant slow-down in the rate of real growth of my regular budget proposals. While the initial budget estimates for the previous and current bienniums provided for rates of real increase of 3.5 and 2.2 per cent respectively, the initial estimates for the 1980–1981 biennium have been limited to a real growth rate of less than 1 per cent.

The increasing financial burden imposed on Member States requires that we preserve and succeed in our efforts to achieve budgetary restraint as well as the most effective utilization of resources through their redeployment, as appropriate, and a rearrangement of priorities. The results of these efforts are reflected in the proposed programme budget for 1980–1981, which has been predicated on extensive redeployment of resources and in which a significant number of new activities are to be financed out of the resources released as a result of the completion or discontinuation of old activities. I believe the results of this first stage in the introduction of the programme monitoring system are encouraging and I intend therefore to extend it at the various levels of programme and resource management.

Difficulties continue to be experienced in the financing of peace-keeping operations, the contributions for which – whether assessed or voluntary – have been insufficient to meet their continuing costs. Troop-contributing countries are not being reimbursed on a current and full basis in accordance with the rates agreed upon. They have conveyed to me their very serious concern over this situation, which places a heavy burden on their Governments. It is becoming clear that the continuation of this trend may make it difficult or impossible for some troop-contributing countries with smaller resources to participate in peace-keeping operations; this in turn may militate against the important principle of equitable geographical distribution in the composition of peace-keeping forces. In any case, as a matter of equity, it is not acceptable that the burden of the peace-keeping operations of the United Nations should fall so heavily on a small group of States which have voluntarily undertaken the responsibility for providing contingents for these operations.

An important question of principle is involved here. The maintenance of international peace and security is a collective responsibility, which should be borne by all States Members of the United Nations.

I therefore appeal to all Governments to give the United Nations peace-keeping operations all possible financial support. In particular, I appeal to those Member States which have not paid their assessments to reconsider their position.

XIII

Until the present time, for a variety of complex political reasons, it has usually proved difficult, if not impossible, for the international community to take positive actions in advance of events. On the political side especially, the time for concerted action has tended to come only when conflict or disaster is imminent or has already occurred. The actions of the international community have often been more in the nature of curative or palliative reactions rather than of bold initiatives to forestall problems or to make better arrangements for the future. This tendency has limited the possibilities of the United Nations as an instrument for concerting the policies of Member States towards constructive goals.

It is not enough to await new – and unthinkable – global disasters in order to bring about a new phase in international relations – a phase of concerted statesmanship positively oriented towards the future rather than dominated by, and reacting to, events and conditions from the past.

Obviously the primary objective of the United Nations must remain the survival of the human race and its environment in the best possible conditions. But this effort is likely in the end to be abortive, unless at the same time we progressively build up the working elements of a global civilization and order unprecedentedly wide in its scope and diversity. This will require, among other things, increasingly effective institutions, the universal acceptance of a minimum basic code of international conduct, and a steady growth of the civility, trust and respect with which nations, as well as individuals, deal with each other. If these aims could be achieved, many doors now closed to progress would be opened, and many precious resources, both human and material, could be used in more constructive and useful ways.

Excessive parochialism can be a dangerous and wasteful force in international as well as national affairs. The United Nations is unique in providing a place where national interests can be articulated, group interests identified and global interests distilled and worked for. If national and group interests can interact in the United Nations within this third dimension of global priorities and with a determination to get real results, it should be possible to move forward steadily on many of the great issues where we now seem to be becalmed.

There are many positive elements which should encourage such a process. Despite the unprecedented level and destructive capacity of armaments, there appears to be a general determination to avoid a third world war. We have the instruments and understanding, in the United Nations and outside it, to carry out these intentions if there is the will to do so. The age of colonial domination, in the classic sense of the term, is over, and instead we have a world of independent nations. We have a technological capacity undreamed of 30 years years ago. We have a new understanding and awareness of the nature of our economic and social problems and of the generation of global problems which are in some measure the result of technological revolution. And we have at least some of the instruments which might be used to deal with them. Racism and prejudice have dwindled and are everywhere under attack. The concept of human rights is becoming an important factor in the life of humanity. New methods of conflict control, such as United Nations peace-keeping, have emerged and have proved their value. There is a determined effort to attack poverty and inequity on a global scale.

In the presence of such undoubted gains, it is worth considering why there is a prevalent mood of anxiety and even bewilderment. Why do Governments continue, often in contravention of the Charter, to take shelter in narrow, nationalistic policies and to use the means provided in the Charter only as a last resort when they find themselves facing impossible risks? It is clear that a lack of mutual confidence and good faith still prevents the 151 Governments which have agreed to abide by the Charter from making it work as intended.

I believe that we are now witnessing some signs of a growing mutual confidence and good faith, often originating in working relationships on difficult issues here at the United Nations. This is an essential element for a move forward from the present age of doubt and anxiety to a new and more generous period of statesmanship. There is nothing basically wrong with the existing international mechanism except the apparent inability of Governments to use it to its full potential. For that to happen, we need to develop a confidence in, and a vision of, the future which is not incessantly clouded or neutralized by narrow aims or temporary setbacks. With confidence and vision the United Nations is capable of becoming a decisive instrument in human development.

The days of national supremacy appear to be over. The community of nations, at the outset of a new era, faces the test of an uncertain future. The United Nations was set up to help all Governments to meet that test together. I hope that the Organization will be used increasingly to build the confidence and develop the vision necessary to guarantee the future.

11 September 1979

KURT WALDHEIM
Secretary-General

INDEX